S U S

FOLK
TALES

Mike O'Leary.

S. Eat

SUSSEX
FOLK
TALES

MICHAEL O'LEARY

ILLUSTRATED BY SU EATON

The
History
Press

To Sarah, Daniel and Ruth,
whose travels have taken them all a bit further than Sussex

And for my mum,
remembering her and her parents when they lived
in Robin Cottage

First published 2013

The History Press
The Mill, Brimscombe Port
Stroud, Gloucestershire, GL5 2QG
www.thehistorypress.co.uk

British Library Cataloguing in Publication Data.
A catalogue record for this book is available from the British Library.

ISBN 978 0 7524 7469 4

Typesetting and origination by The History Press
Printed in Great Britain

CONTENTS

Acknowledgements

Thank you to Rosie and Ben Sutcliffe for being such excellent walking companions on many an exploration, and for sharing my geographical mania and juvenile humour!

Thank you to Pat Bowen for her help and hospitality, and for generously sharing a story, and potentially more. Her love of Sussex is infectious.

Thank you to Sarah Rundle for being so helpful and generous with information, and for her research and suggestions. Sarah is a real, sharing storyteller.

Thank you to Umi Sinha for drawing my attention to Ovingdean Grange via the story of the Devil's Dyke as related by an entirely fictitious Master Cisbury Oldfirle! Thanks also to Umi for the chance to tell a few tales at the Guesthouse Storytellers in Newhaven.

Thank you to Jamie Crawford, another selfless storyteller, for suggesting all this.

Thank you to the driven O'Donnell for a conversation about the Mixon Hole, as we sat outside a pub in Stromness!

Thank you to Baljinder and Aran for story suggestions whilst I wrote some of this in a courtyard in Patiala.

Thank you to all at the History Press.

And, of course, thanks to all the people I've bumped into in my wanderings; the bloke in the pub, the woman in the farm shop, the kids in the schools from Selsey Bill to Crawley, and whoever the hell that was in Brighton. Stories are being spun all the time.

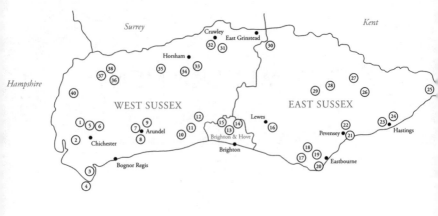

39 ↓

Legend to O'Leary's rough map of Sussex, showing story locations

THE SEVEN GOOD
THINGS OF SUSSEX

Pulborough eel
Selsey cockle
Chichester lobster
Rye herring
Arundel mullet
Amberley trout
Bourne wheatear

INTRODUCTION

When I was asked to tell stories at a place called Gumber Bothy, I thought it must be somewhere in the Scottish Highlands. However, I soon discovered that it was in West Sussex and close to home. I drove off to a deserted car park up on the South Downs, where I was met by a teacher who led me to Gumber Bothy, some way from the road. My job was to tell stories to somewhat disaffected teenagers around a campfire.

I dragged my story box behind me, a converted ammunition box that I'd found on a dump, that had since grown wheels, and which contained various musical instruments and artefacts that sometimes help a story along. Swords to ploughshares.

The session went well; there's nothing like a fire, the open air, and a few tales to temporarily dispel disaffection, and then it was time for me to head back to my van. The teacher asked me if I needed to be shown the way, or whether I could find my own way back.

'I'll find my own way back, no problem,' I said, full of male direction-finding confidence – and off I plodded, story box trundling behind me.

Of course – I got lost.

I stood on a hill, tired and weary, my hand hurting from hauling on the rope that pulled my story box, and looked out into the darkness. There were no lights, not a single one. Yet this was the south of England – so surely there's always a light somewhere; a house, a farm, a stretch of road with a car. But there was nothing; just the smudge of woodland under a pale quarter moon, and the sweep of the Downs.

I eventually found my way back to the van, but only after realising how wild parts of the southern counties can be. Arguably, Sussex, east and west combined, may contain more woodland than any other English county. To find out for sure would involve someone having to count every tree – and it would be extremely frustrating to lose count at 999,999 and have to start all over again – but there is an awful lot of non-urban land. In the woods, and out on the Downs, it can be wild.

'As night falls, it requires very little effort for those who stand beside a downland tumulus in the screaming wind, or in the dark recesses of a wealden copse, to feel something of the religion of the pagan South Saxons, their belief in barrow wights, witch hounds and wood demons,' wrote an unknown author very evocatively, and up on the Downs, for downs are always up, it can be wild.

(I love the above quote, but I am unable to properly attribute the author, something that is my fault. In the early part of this century I was involved in a storytelling project in mid-Sussex.

I photocopied a chapter, called Pagan Sussex, out of a library book, but neglected to write down the name of the author. My recent enquiries, and twiddlings with Google, have failed to locate the book, which is no longer in the library, so if anyone could identify it, I would be grateful.)

Our wander through Sussex, however, will not just be through those wild regions – we'll also take a stroll through the urban landscape, and the semi-urban landscape: the 'edgelands'. We'll find stories in Brighton, Crawley and Gatwick, as well as the more conventionally picturesque Arundel or Lewes.

I have been unable to resist the temptation to number the chapters according to the way Sussex shepherds used to count (or tell) sheep, though they really were counting the sheep in pairs. There are variations of this, but I have taken this list from the Revd W.D. Parish's *Dictionary of the Sussex Dialect*, 1875:

1. One-erum	6. Sath-erum
2. Two-erum	7. Wineberry
3. Cock-erum	8. Wagtail
4. Shu-erum	9. Tarry-diddle
5. Sith-erum	10. Den

Maybe it is sad that I got this list from a book, rather than from a shepherd, but when I tried I nearly got run over by a quad bike.

The book is ordered geographically – we shall wander from the west to the east through southern Sussex, and then circle back westwards through northern Sussex. Circling. The old stories say that if you circle a church 'widdershins' – anti-clockwise – the Devil may appear. If you should circle that wondrous Sussex landmark, Chanctonbury Ring, he'll almost certainly put in an appearance. Oh dear – and I'm suggesting that we circle the entire county of Sussex widdershins, picking up stories as we go. I hope that we survive to tell the tale.

In Sussex, if it's not the Devil that makes an appearance, then it's likely to be a dragon. Let us start walking.

ONE-ERUM

FROM A HILL TO A BILL THROUGH A HOLE

Sussex is full of dragons – the evidence for this is to be found in the pub names: George and Dragon, Red Dragon, Green Dragon, plain and simple Dragon; there is even a village called Dragons Green. To some folklorists these dragons are relics of the ancient 'Celtic' past (I put the word 'Celtic' in inverted commas because it is a vague and rather romantic word generally used by people with an excessive fondness for ambient music), whilst some say they are relics of a more recent Saxon past (the name Sussex means 'Land of the South Saxons'). Others say that the dragon is a symbol from medieval Christianity. I'm not a folklorist, I'm just a slightly tipsy storyteller, so I wouldn't know – I am, however, rather suspicious of overarching theories of everything, and 'dragon' is a word, and words can attach themselves to many things, whilst ideas and beliefs can evolve, change, morph and merge. It may of course simply be that there used to be a lot of dragons in Sussex.

(I wish, however, to become a serious folklorist, and intend to begin my research by visiting every pub in Sussex with the word 'dragon' in the name. I am willing to accept a research grant from anyone who wishes to further understand this important topic.)

Our widdershins perambulation through Sussex begins by crossing the border from Hampshire and coming to a truly wondrous though not particularly well known place called Kingley Vale. I am eternally grateful to Nick Howes, a teacher at Funtington Primary School, who told me about the Vale when I was telling stories at the school. When I had finished that particular storytelling session I took a stroll up to Kingley Vale, and found that it was a national nature reserve. I wandered through woodland into a narrow, steeply ascending valley, and the birdsong from the woods on each side came to me like a sort of stereo; different sounds for each ear.

Then I entered the ancient yew wood. I've seen yew forests before, but nothing like this. A forest usually causes trees to be taller and thinner because of the competition for sunlight, but the trees here are the size of churchyard yews, and there are many of them. Within the trees there is the silent atmosphere of a cathedral, and an intense feeling of being watched. All the trees seem to have grotesque faces, and sometimes these are not seen at the time, but only on photos downloaded afterwards.

After leaving the yew wood I took a steep climb up Bow Hill, on the ridge of which there are four Neolithic round barrows known as the Devil's Humps (also known as the Kings' Graves and Bow Hill Barrows), plus a number of smaller barrows. These look for all the world like a line of scales along a dragon's back. From this dragon's back there is a spectacular view across the coastal plain, and way over to the Isle of Wight, as well as a fine view north over the South Downs.

Dragon Scales and Dragon Blood

In the ninth century, a party of Danes from the Danelaw of the North decided to attack Chichester. They landed at Bosham, destroyed the town, and left a trail of misery and destruction behind them as they headed north, intent on circling Chichester and taking it from the rear, something these Vikings were rather fond of doing. They were wary of Saxon defenders from

Chichester, so they marched under cover of darkness. They found themselves entering Kingley Vale and headed up towards Bow Hill for what would be a great offensive point behind the city.

As they entered the stillness of the yew forest, however, the weather seemed to change and the temperature dropped. A mist rolled through the Devil's Humps and spilled down the crevice of Kingley Vale – whispering, murmuring and swirling into the forest of yews. The faces of the trees grinned at the Danes, and then something began to detach itself from the hill.

Or was the mist in the minds of the Vikings? They had travelled seas, followed coasts and stars, and gazed into an infinity of sky. Yet, at the same time, all that filled their minds was the prospect of rape, pillage and a crude Valhalla. Their motivation was a sense of competition with each other, an intense fear of being made to look less than a man by a competitor with whom it was necessary to cooperate. Their minds were dominated by feuds and threats to their 'honour'.

The mist from the Devil's Humps and the yew grove entered their minds and took on the shape of the Vikings' own symbol, the symbol of the dragon – a symbol designed to strike fear into the hearts of their victims, a symbol carved on the prows of their dragon ships – and turned it against them. Up on Bow Hill the dragon seemed to tear its body from the ground, rip its claws out of the Sussex chalk, and slink, burning and hissing, down the hill. The Danes felt the dragon all around them, and turned on each other, screaming their battle cries, and hacked with sword and axe. Each war cry belonged to a family, a dynasty; each warrior believed his war cry to be superior to the others, and every shout and scream was a provocation. For an hour, amidst the grinning trees, they tore each other apart, until the ground ran with blood, and the birds outside the grove began to sing the dawn chorus.

The story goes that the memory of their deaths haunts the yew grove, and that the memory of a dragon stretches across Bow Hill.

If you go to the yew grove in Kingley Vale, you will find sharp pieces of yew bark, as hard and sharp as dragon scales, and underneath them you will find the sap of the yew tree, which is as thick and red as arterial blood.

The Bells of Bosham

News of the defeat at Kingley Vale failed to reach the Danelaw, because there were no survivors left to tell the tale. There were many reasons why a longship wouldn't return, not least the strong possibility of being wrecked along the coast – the arrival of another fleet of longships along the coast of Sussex was less to do with discovering the fate of those who perished at Kingley Vale, and more to do with rumours of rich pickings at Chichester, and the prosperous port of Bosham.

Watchers on the coast of Selsey saw the dragon ships, striped sails a-flapping, ply their way around Selsey Bill, and into the creeks, channels and lagoons where Bosham hides. Hidden and sheltered though Bosham may be, it was a thriving port, with a church and a monastery, both of which contained treasures that had travelled along maritime trade routes from all over Europe. When news of the imminent arrival of the Vikings reached the populace, everyone – monks, farmers, tradesmen and their families – upped and fled, heading inland into the forest and up to the Downs.

The Vikings sacked the town, and then gleefully looted the largest bell from the church. What a prize! Not only valuable, but a symbol of the church; to take it was to emasculate the town and leave a mark of power. They lowered the bell into the largest longboat, which sank down until its gunwales were just above the water – the Vikings were willing to risk the boat swamping and carrying them to a watery Valhalla, in order to bring such a great prize back to the Danelaw.

As the dragon ships pulled out of Bosham Channel, through the creeks and inlets and towards the open sea, a group of monks – those with the special knowledge of the ring o'bells – ran back into the church, and, with the remaining bells, started to ring a backwards peal in a way that only their order knew. A sudden squall kicked up, a flurry of cats' paws became a confusion of waves, the wind seemed to blow from every which way, and the low-lying dragon ship was swamped. The huge bell broke free, and with a great sonorous peal, crashed through the side of the boat. The Viking ship sank, and as it did so, a whirlpool span round and round, and, to the sound of the pealing bells of Bosham, the other ships span into the maelstrom and disappeared.

There was no way to retrieve the bell, and so there it lay, and it lies there still.

There was, however, an attempt to retrieve it, several hundred years after it sank.

The story begins when a Bosham fishing boat netted a merman. He was more seal than man, and more man than seal, and he gawped at them and tried to jump back into the sea, but they tied him down, gasping and gulping, and took him back to Bosham to be prodded and poked, examined and tweaked, and finally shut into a cold cell under the church.

Then, one cold misty evening, the monks rang the church bells to announce vespers, and from the deep beyond the inlet came a booming reply. Every time the monks rang the changes, the bell replied from the sea. In his cell under the church, the man from the sea started to gibber and shriek and rattle his chains.

'Can we get the bell back?' thought the monks.

'Can we get the bell back?' echoed the people of Bosham.

'Bell back, bell back,' gibbered the merman, and the people came and took him from his cell, and, in his chains, took him back out to sea, back out to the echoing bell.

They gave him a net to contain the bell, but kept a chain fastened to his leg so he couldn't escape. Way down below, he completed his task and so they hauled him up. They then tried to haul up the bell, but nearly swamped the boats in the process. Finally they fastened ropes to the nets, and ran the ropes to six white oxen on shore. It is well known that only white oxen can haul a bell from the deep – just ask the men of Knowlton in Dorset, or the folk of Etchingham in East Sussex. The oxen hauled and hauled, but just as one of the monks noticed that an ox had a black hair on its rump, the man from the sea howled, a squall blew up, and the boat capsized. The net tore, there was a 'crack' as the shackles holding the merman snapped, and boat, crew and merman were pitched into the sea, and the bell 'BONG BONG BONGED' its way back down into the depths.

Some men were drowned, some were hauled out of the water – but the merman was free again. As for the bell, it is said that sometimes when the church bells of Bosham ring out on a misty-moisty evening, a deep reply can be heard from across the harbour, and the reply completes the proper ring o'bells.

It is also said that a yacht may make its way into the harbour on such a still, misty evening, and that the man on board – the banker, or TV producer, or whoever it is – must keep a careful eye out. For it could be that a merman hauls himself aboard, and it may be that the woman of the boat finds the salty embraces of the man from the sea more enticing than those of the jaded money man.

THE MERMAN FIGURINE

Bosham is vulnerable to flooding, and there is now a sophisticated system of pipes and sluice gates in place as flood control. I was told that during the digging of the trenches for the pipes, a little figurine – half man, half fish – was unearthed, but I don't know what became of it. I did, of course, receive this information from that impeccable source: a bloke who heard it from a bloke. Strangely, though, I heard personally, from the rather enigmatic diver O'Donnell, that whilst diving Bell Hole, out in the Bosham Deeps, he also found such a figurine. O'Donnell is, however, a professional diver, and divers do tend to be great storytellers. I'm never inclined to entirely trust a storyteller.

THE BOSHAM CAR WASH

Strange place, Bosham, not least for the pronunciation – 'Bozzum' – but then why should spellings and pronunciation go together? It would deny the history of the language and make life too easy for foreigners.

One of the strange things about Bosham is the car wash. If you want to wash your car whilst there you can participate in a piece of modern folklore – for folklore is not something that sits statically in the past; after all, the present is always drifting back into the past, just as the future drifts back to the present!

Take your car down to the road by the beach, at the end of the High Street, down by Bosham Quay. Park it there; it's a lovely spot for gazing out over Bosham Channel. Ignore, as so many do, the sign that says 'This Road Floods Each Tide' and wander off to the pub for a few drinks. You can drink as much as you like, because you won't be driving afterwards; a tidal car wash really doesn't help a car's engine function effectively. The Bosham Car Wash will be in folklore collections of the future, but I'm all for watching folklore as it happens. If you put 'Bosham Car Wash' into YouTube, modern folklore will display itself in front of your eyes, and you can enjoy it (as long as it's not your car).

CANUTE'S DAUGHTER

And what of the church from whence the Danes stole the bell? Holy Trinity Church is flooded with history. It is depicted on the Bayeux Tapestry; Harold sailed from here to meet William of Normandy in 1064. I don't think the meeting went well.

King Canute is said to be buried here, and he had a palace, now gone, in Bosham. There is a legend that it was in Bosham that he demonstrated the limits of a king's power to his sycophantic courtiers, by commanding the tide to retreat. However, that event actually took place over the border in Hampshire; at least I said so in *Hampshire and Isle of Wight Folk Tales*, and if I change my mind I'm bound to upset someone.

Canute was, of course – as he would have to have been in those times – a thug and a warlord, and his real name was Cnut, which suits him much better.

He did, however, have a little daughter and she was everything that her father wasn't. She was kind and caring; she insisted that no one in Bosham should ever go hungry. She was a delight to the village. All of Bosham was in mourning when, at the age of eight, she slipped and fell into the mill stream. She was buried under Holy Trinity Church, and after a while history slipped into legend, and no one really knew if the body of Canute's daughter lay under the church or not.

Then, in 1865, the church underwent a restoration. The vicar took the opportunity to investigate the legend. The floor was taken up, and a stone coffin was found. It was opened, and there were the remains of a child. As they removed the heavy stone lid, it broke in half with a crack. There was a rush of air, and something flew from the coffin like a whisper.

The next day a little girl arrived at a nearby farm. She carried a jug, and held it out to the farmer's wife.

'Do you want milk, dear?' said the farmer's wife, surprised to see a girl that she didn't recognise. The girl didn't reply. She just smiled.

'That'll be a penny, dear,' said the good woman, after filling the jug, but the girl, still smiling, just turned and walked away.

The farmer's wife just gaped, and she was so beguiled by the girl's smile that she didn't chase after her.

The smiling child returned the next day and once more held up the jug.

'My dear, it does cost a penny,' said the good woman, but once again the girl turned and walked away, carrying a full jug of milk.

There is, of course, a third time, because things usually happen in threes in stories; that is if it's not sevens, and the listeners usually get impatient before the storyteller reaches the seventh event.

The third time, after filling the jug, the farmer's wife decided to follow the girl. Into the village they went, down along the water's edge, until the little girl entered the churchyard and disappeared behind a gravestone. When the farmer's wife looked behind the gravestone, what did she see, to her surprise and consternation, but the little girl holding a baby and feeding it milk from the tip of her finger.

'Oh my dear little mite,' said the woman, gathering up the baby. In a whisper the girl seemed to go from them, leaving no trace, and yet some trace, like a blessing.

Well, the abandoned baby was a girl, and she was brought up by the farmer and his wife, who had never had children. When she was an adult she emigrated to Newfoundland, and it was her great-granddaughter who told me the story as we went fishing for cod out of Newfoundland's Fortune Harbour.

As for the stone coffin, it was re-excavated in 1954, and no bones were found. What was found, however, was a small bottle containing a strange brown liquid. No one was able to work out what the liquid was; but I know. It's the story (stories can keep for a long time when they're bottled, but you always need to let them out in the end).

The Man in the Moon

Children can be great sources of modern folklore, not least because they don't call it folklore and put it in books. It's just stuff. They'll tell you about Bloody Mary who haunts the school toilets, or the ghastly, ghostly teacher who haunts the caretaker's treasure trove of a cupboard. It was children in Selsey Bill who told me about Patrick Moore.

Well, Patrick Moore is a legend because of all those years in the public eye as a popular astronomer, and because of his individuality (something that people sometimes call 'eccentricity', but I don't really know what that word means). He certainly lives in Selsey, and amongst his many accomplishments, a local feat is that he played a key role in founding the Bognor Birdman competition, where people attempt to fly off the end of Bognor pier. It's all in aid of charity, and I don't know if anyone has yet succeeded in taking flight.

The story that children tell is that he has been to the moon. In 1998 Patrick Moore was eating in his local Indian restaurant when there was an explosive thunderclap. Across Selsey, windows were sucked from their frames, cars were lifted into the air, and chimney stacks crashed to the ground. The tornado, for this really was a 'twister', whirled the restaurant around and around and hurled Sir Patrick up to the moon. For two years Patrick Moore was the man in the moon – and who else would he be – until the year 2000, when he descended unto earth in another twister, and arrived back in his own shower. The children said that this was the reason that nothing was heard from Patrick Moore between 1998 and 2000, and I rather regret having checked this out and finding it not to be true. Still, Sir Patrick himself said, 'I can't explain it. It is said that lightning never strikes twice, but clearly the same is not true of tornados. It makes me quite nervous to go outside.'

(Since I wrote this, Patrick Moore has died. He has left a Patrick Moore-sized hole in Selsey, but he'll go on being a legend.)

THE MIXON HOLE

At one time you would have to be careful about going outside at night in the area where Selsey is now. This was because of the smugglers.

That is, unless you were dead.

An old custom was that the dead should be placed, in their coffins, on the shingle beach at what was then wild land at the end of the misty and remote Manhood Peninsula. In the morning the coffin would be gone – and it was said that the people of the sea had taken it to the Mixon Hole.

Now, over time, the sea has claimed much of the coastline, and where the Mixon Hole lies on the seabed – now a challenging focus for divers – there was once a river estuary, a Roman fort, and a straight Roman road that led to Fishbourne Palace, near Chichester. Fishermen have always known about the Mixon Hole, because it's a good spot for lobsters, and it always carried the story of a lost settlement.

However, it was also possible that the leaving of a coffin was a smuggler's ploy, and that the coffin contained contraband goods to be picked up by a coastal cutter and distributed up and down the coast.

And so one evening a revenue officer followed the funeral procession down to the shingle beach, watched the coffin being laid to rest, watched the mourners depart … and waited.

Night fell, and with a moon flying behind ragged clouds, still he waited, fortifying himself with the occasional swig from a brandy flask.

No doubt the brandy had been smuggled, but a job is a job; catch a smuggling gang and you'd make a name for yourself, and get a promotion.

Then, in the early hours of the morning, his blood ran cold. Out of the sea there came first heads – then shoulders – then torsos – then whole bodies – six creatures, or men, or monsters. Two looked like Roman soldiers, and four like drowned mariners – and for the love of God, wasn't one of them old Samuel Stacker from Bosham, who had been drowned only the year before? There were limpet shells on their faces and their bodies were festooned with seaweed and sea wrack and their eyes shone in the darkness like pale, yellow lanterns.

They stooped over the coffin, lifted it onto their shoulders, and walked back into the sea. The astonished excise man followed them, and his astonishment turned to wonder when he saw steps descending and a straight road cut through the sea.

A voice drifted back to him through the night air, or was it through the water; 'Do you see yonder excise man that be following us?'

'Aye, I do.'

'What shall we do?'

'Let him take his soul down to the Mixon Hole.'

And so he did: excise man, soul and all, followed them to a four square fort and after the coffinbearers had entered, he came to the gate and the guards let him pass; for he'd abandoned any pretence at hiding.

Inside the castle, on thrones of seaweed and sea shells, sat the king and queen of the Mixon Hole, whilst around them swam tompot blennies, gobies and blobfish, none of them a pretty sight.

'Well,' said the king, 'share the rest of your brandy, for we have plenty more.'

And so he did – and a drowned musician picked up his barnacle-encrusted harp, and another his flute, and they began to play. The king began to dance, and so did the queen, and so did the revenue officer.

> The cod and the hake,
> The haddock and the sole,
> They all danced together,
> Down the Mixon Hole.

Then the king and queen's daughter began to dance, and oh she was a beautiful mermaid – all wibbly-wobbly green flesh, double bubble chins, and flashing fish scales.

And she gazed at the revenue officer and said, 'Stay – stay with me.' And he said 'yes', and then he thought of his wife and children, and he said 'no', and then he thought of the rippling flesh of the sea princess, and he said 'yes', and then he thought of promotion and a life in London and said 'no', and then he thought of the sea, and green caverns, and salty caresses, and said 'yes', and then he shouted 'NO!', and ran back to the straight road through the sea, and the steps to the beach – it was morning and he was back on shore. But it wasn't familiar; there was a straight sea wall that seemed to be carved out of stone, and when he climbed onto it there were weird houses from a bad dream, and people wearing strange clothes. A man approached, with a dog on a long, leather cord. The excise man spoke to him, asking what was what, and the man looked frightened and hurried away. Then there was a youth, wearing a hood, and with shoes that shone white.

'Where be I?' asked the excise man.

'You is a nutter, innit,' replied the youth, and also turned away, shouting incomprehensible things over his shoulder.

Well, the revenue officer could not account for anyone putting the clocks forward to this extent, and he wandered Selsey for a while, got picked up by the police, was sectioned and released, and now he wanders the streets of Brighton telling his tale. In Brighton there are people who believe him, because in Brighton there are people who like to chemically alter their brains. I also believe him, though, and that is because I have talked to the diver O'Donnell, who dived the Mixon Hole when the weather was inclement and the tide was turning. He said that at the right angle you could feel yourself flying over a fort and an estuary, and you could see the Roman ships a-coming into harbour. In spite of the fact the bird we call a 'diver' is known to the Americans as a 'loon', I know that the Mixon Hole carries a memory, and that land and seabed carry memories in exactly the same way our brains do; because where do we come from, if not the land and the sea; and where do they come from, if not the stars?

Pook Lane

Before we wander out of this chapter and over an entirely arbitrary border into the next chapter, let's say a word or two about the Sussex fairies, who we'll be seeing more of later.

In Sussex people called them 'Pharisees', and David Arscott, in *The Little Book of Sussex*, says this comes from what's known to grammarians as 'the replicated plural' – once common in the county's speech. School teachers would attempt to drum the habit out of the children by getting them to recite a bit of nonsense verse:

> I saw three ghosteses sitting on posteses,
> Eating hot toastesses.
> The butter ran down their fisteses,
> Dirty little beastesses!

The term 'Pharisees' also allowed people to give the fairies a biblical connection – some say that they are fallen angels. Esther Meynell wrote, in 1947: 'few of the old Sussex people would dream of using such an 'outland' word [as] ... fairies ... it is as Pharisees they are known.'

Just north of Chichester, just south-east of Kingley Vale, and just west of the next chapter, there is a village called East Lavant, and in East Lavant there is a lane called Pook Lane, and in Pook Lane there are Pharisees, and they are Pharisees of not very friendly intent.

Now, there are Pook Lanes throughout Sussex and Hampshire, and they always seem to be associated with the 'other' people (Kipling used the name in his Sussex-based book *Puck of Pook's Hill*), maybe because 'puca' or 'pucel' is an Old English word for 'goblin', and the fairies aren't just little, fluttery things; they are a lot of strange creatures, who if not downright malignant, are at the very least amoral.

Now, I'm sure most civilised people will own a copy of Ronald Edward Zupko's *A Dictionary of Weights and Measures for the British Isles: The Middle Ages to the Twentieth Century*. Certainly the Secretary of State for Education should send a copy to every school, and children should learn to recite the entire book. If you turn to p. 308 in your copy you will see that a poke, poik, pok, puka or pokeputte is a sack, usually used for carrying wool – and didn't the Pharisees love to carry their sacks down Pook Lane. Often they'd steal something; for instance, a pig (hence the term 'pig in a poke', but that's a story we'll come to later), and they would lure unwary travellers down Pook Lane to steal their horses and carts, and load their belongings into their pokeputtes. One farmer, Peter Parker, was found in the morning, minus his horse and cart, and the cart was found later, tipped into the River Lavant, where those Pharisees must have left it after their wild, nocturnal ride. Maybe this is what happened in 2010, when a five-year-old boy clambered into his father's Mitsubishi Shogun and started to play about with it in a manner that was really very intelligent for a little boy. The car took off and travelled for four miles with the little boy standing up, the top of his head just visible to startled passing motorists, desperately steering the car to avoid collisions, eventually crashing into the wall of Cynthia Rivett's house in Pook Lane. It was the fairies, of course, who caused it to happen – and a brave little boy battling against them.

THE TRUNDLE

Overlooking all this is a remarkable hill called the Trundle. Underneath the Trundle it is said there is buried a golden calf, though some say it's a golden horse. This might be why the fairies hold their racing meets up on the hill, and drink, bet, fight, and generally cause mayhem in miniature. Woe betide you, though, should you see them – for they'll poke out your eyes. Some people, who may deserve to have their eyes poked out, take folding chairs and binoculars to the top of the Trundle, and watch the races at Goodwood, for the race track is just below. I can never understand this, for what is the point of the races if you can't get drunk and lose a few quid? Still, there's a great view from the top of the Trundle, way out across Chichester Harbour to the creeks and inlets around Bosham and Selsey, over to the Isle of Wight, across to the yew woods around Kingley Vale, and eastwards over the rolling chalk Downs. We'll head that way for the next chapter.

Arundel and up the Arun to Amberley

(Starting with Stuff)

If you are travelling eastwards out of the last chapter and along the A27 you will see Arundel on your left, and the castle and cathedral up on the hill is a striking sight. A town dominated by a castle on a hill almost looks more French or Luxembourgish than English.

Should you go into the castle you will find that it is a veritable cornucopia of stuff – crowns, coronets, tables, chairs, pictures, statues, statuettes, scrolls, sceptres, bits of armour, furniture that Queen Victoria looked at, sat on, slept in once – the list is endless. Were all this stuff to be found in the home of someone who was not a member of the upper classes, one would hope that a benign army of declutterers and a skip might come in and help the unhappy inhabitant get sorted.

If you navigate your way through this tastefully presented mass of stuff, you will come to the armoury. More stuff! The sort of stuff that generations of people have used to inflict pain and misery on each other. Amidst these weapons, there is a huge, ancient-looking sword. The label says: 'MONGLEY. Large two edged sword, probably English work of early fourteenth century. Bladesmith's mark of a cross within a shield. Traditionally said to have belonged to the legendary hero Lord Bevis of Hamtun, Quondam constable of Arundel Castle.' This is Mortglay, the sword of the mighty giant Bevis, and I was recently told off for photographing it. I had to photograph it, and touch it, because it had featured so often in stories I'd told over the years that it had become as magical a symbol to me as Excalibur is to so many.

Should you read *Hampshire and Isle of Wight Folk Tales* by that renowned folklorist, Michael O'Leary, you will discover that in Southampton the stories tell that a Hampshire dragon hurled the sword Mortglay from Southampton to Arundel. All along the south coast there are relics of someone called Bevis; he's in the landscape of the area as much as Arthur is in the landscape of England and Wales. In Southampton he is often called Bevois, because that was the name given him in a medieval romance that set the story in Southampton, and in the city there are areas known as Bevois Town and Bevois Valley. Further east, and nearer Sussex, on the top of Portsdown Hill (that singular hill that overlooks Portsmouth), there is a long barrow called Bevis's Grave, and on the border between Hampshire and Sussex there is a long barrow called Bevis's Thumb. The Hampshire stories differ somewhat from the Sussex ones; in Hampshire, Bevis is a knight who is accompanied by a giant called Ascupart, whereas in Sussex Bevis is himself the giant. This may be because the medieval romancers extended folklore, or maybe because folk simplified the medieval romance. Folklorists could write papers on this, extrapolating back to the true and original source, but I think it may be that stories fragment, morph, merge, gain complexity, lose complexity, mate with other stories and produce offspring, expire, explode, and take roads to nowhere and somewhere. I like to call this the 'Fart in a Colander' theory, but its more mundane title is chaos theory.

BEVIS OF ARUNDEL

The story begins in the time of giants that superseded the time of dragons. The giants had driven the dragons from the land, not by guile and cunning, but by chucking rocks at them. The dragon that had squatted hissing and steaming on the hill above Arundel had hurled itself, screaming, into a bottomless pool at Lyminster, which is an entrance to the other world. He was to emerge periodically, but we'll hear about that later.

So the giant Bevis sat on a rock overlooking the River Arun and watched the world change, whilst he picked the dry skin from between his toes and skimmed stones across to the Isle of Wight. He watched the river flow to the sea in times of rain and times of drought. He watched the people paddle up the river; the little dark people in Neolithic times, the Romans, the Belgae, the various Jutes and Saxons. He watched the clearings being made in the forest, and the smoke trailing up into the sky from the settlement fires. He watched cultures change, and as often as not it was the people adapting to a new cultural wave, rather than an actual new wave of people.

Then it was the time of the Normans, and they built a castle, and Bevis adapted by becoming its guardian, sitting by the main gate pulling faces at anyone who looked like trouble. For this less-than-onerous task he was given a whole ox every week, plus two hogsheads of beer, all of which he consumed with bread and mustard. This continued into the medieval period, though no one called it the medieval period, for everyone believes that now is always now.

The old stories relate that Bevis would periodically wade across to the Isle of Wight, but they never say why. These are stories that are found in Sussex, but no tales from the Isle of Wight tell of the incoming giant Bevis, though they have their own giants. It falls to me to expose the real truth about Bevis's sub-aquatic adventures.

He would wade in the general direction of the Isle of Wight until his head sank beneath the waves – but he would never arrive. The truth is that he was heading for the Mixon Hole, where he had an assignation with the beautiful, green, wibbly-wobbly princess that dwelt therein.

It is sad to relate, though, that from the princess's point of view, it was just lust. She had a thing for giants, and Bevis – big, silly, soft-hearted Bevis – was just one amongst many. But Bevis – poor Bevis – believed that he'd fallen in love, and if he believed he'd fallen in love, why then, so he had.

One day, amidst the green caverns of the Mixon Hole, before they got down to action, Bevis went down upon bended knee and declared his love.

'Marry me, oh wondrous and wobbly one,' he declared, 'come to Arundel and be my lady. I will build for thee the mightiest fish tank in all Christendom (after reinforcing the castle walls to all appropriate stress factor recommendations), and from there thou shalt survey all of the lands of which thou shalt be lady, for the dukes and duchesses, earls and earlesses, are but names, and 'tis us, the folk of myth and legend, that really rule this land.'

'Oh Christ,' thought the princess of the Mixon Hole, 'he's gone all soft in the head. I can't think of anything worse than marrying him – I never have this trouble with the Cerne Abbas giant.'

'Ah, mighty Bevis,' quoth she, 'thy offer is indeed wondrous, but I belong here, amidst the green caverns, the silver shoals that swim in from the Atlantic, the eddies and tides that do swirl around the sunken rocks and wrecks of the Manhood Peninsula. I am of the sea, and could never live like a prisoner on land.'

'Nice one,' she thought, 'that'll shut him up.' But it didn't.

'Then, oh must-be-married merrymaid,' quoth Bevis, 'I will forsake all that I hold dear on land; I will come and dwell beneath the ocean wave; I will live under the rolling deep, where the scattered waters rave, and the winds their revels keep. I will "take the tail" [a phrase used to describe the adaption to underwater living, often used by fishermen who marry mermaids]; I will be thy merman prince, and when thy father and mother pass on to the subaqueous caverns of glory, you and I will reign as king and queen of the Mixon Hole.'

'Oh my generous and gigantic lover,' she replied, 'it could never be; thou art of the land, and I am of the sea.'

'No, no, please be mine,' he pleaded (always a mistake). 'I cannot live without you. You must be mine.' Finally it was all too much for her – his pleading, his blubbery, teary, moony face, his pathetically beseeching eyes, his runny nose – it all irritated her beyond endurance.

'Do you really think I'd marry you?' she screeched, 'you gurt big, lubberin', stupid giant. Look at you, thick as the Sussex mud and chalk you come from. Okay, you're a bit fit for a touch of the old dalliance, but do you really think I'd want anything to do with you when you go bald and your teeth fall out. Go on, bugger off back to Arundel, and don't come sniffing around here any more.'

Oh Bevis – the crack as his heart broke could be heard up on the South Downs, and it raised a tsunami that demolished the town of Francheville on the Isle of Wight, and knocked down one of the chalk pillars of the Needles.

Blindly, he stumbled back to Arundel and took to his great iron bed. The Earl of Arundel and his lady came to the giant's bedside and pleaded with him to cheer up, and so did the entire population of the castle. But if your heart is broken, the last thing you need is a lot of bloody people telling you to cheer up – and Bevis sought only oblivion.

He lifted his mighty sword Mortglay, and said to the assembled multitude, 'Where e'r this sword landeth, there lay my poor body to rest,' and hurled it out of the window. Then he closed his eyes and died. The people took a team of oxen and hauled the body out to where the sword was sticking out of the ground, and there they buried him. If you should go out to Arundel Park, which is a stretch of countryside behind the castle, you will find Bevis's Tomb, which some people say is a long barrow. You will clearly see that it is the grave of a giant, and this will just as clearly tell you that my story is true. Go and have a look at the sword in the armoury too, but if you don't like being told off, don't take a photograph of it.

THE LYMINSTER KNUCKER

Below Arundel, the A27 does a strange thing; it drops onto a sliproad that leads on to an unfinished stretch of dual carriageway. Anyone heading west would have seen the dual carriageway just come to a stop. Some say the road building was halted because of local opposition, others because of the danger of upsetting a dragon.

You see, if we leave the A27 at this point and trundle down the road to Littlehampton, we come to a village called Lyminster (pronounced Li-minster; they have strange pronunciations in Sussex, Ardingly is pronounced Arding-lie!). In Lyminster there is a church called St Mary Magdalene, and a pathway behind the church leads us past a pond called the Knucker Hole.

The Knucker Hole is now surrounded by chain-link fencing and is used as a private fishing lake – but it feels strange. If you walk past it on a hot day, the temperature seems to drop, and a breeze can blow in from the sea, making the reeds whisper secrets. Sometimes vapours emanate from the pond, and it is said that these vapours can affect the sanity of people living close by, causing them to become as aggressive and insular as a dragon.

If you walk past the pond you come to low-lying fields and a wondrous view up to Arundel; whilst maybe the little train to Littlehampton will rumble past a few fields away. The names of the villages the train might trundle past make a poem: Arundel – Cross Bush – Lyminster – Wick – Rustington – Climbing –

Yapton – Bilsham – Flansham – Felpham – Bognor. But back to the Knucker Hole.

It is said that a dragon lives in the pond. It is called a knucker. Now, knucker is a Sussex word for a dragon, and may well have evolved from the old Saxon word 'Nicor', which means 'water monster'. It may also relate to the word 'knuckle', which is of course a joint on your hand, but the Saxon word 'cnucl' means joint or junction, and can refer to the surface of a pond – when that pond is an entrance to another world. The Knucker Hole must be such a place.

In medieval times the knucker – a terrible worm – dragged itself from the pond and terrorised the nuns who lived nearby. The mighty giant Bevis descended the hill from Arundel, flying on a magical horse, Hirondelle, and fought the knucker for three days and three nights, before driving it back into the pond. It remained there for several hundred years before it was disturbed by the men of Lyminster.

The knucker had passed into legend, but the pond was always reputed to be bottomless and Jim Pulk bet Jim Puttock that no one could ever find the bottom of the pond. Accordingly the two Jims and their cronies took one of the bells from the belfry of St Mary Magdalene, tied it to a bell rope, and lowered it down into the pond. It never touched the bottom, so they got another rope, tied it to the first rope, lowered it further down, and still it never touched the bottom. They got another rope, tied it to the second rope, lowered it further down, and still it never touched the bottom. Then the rope slipped through their fingers and they lost the bell; it plummeted, tolling as it went, down to who knows where. They then got a second bell and tried the same thing, but they lost that one too. Since then, the church at Lyminster has only had six bells; a good number of bells reqired to play a satisfactory 'ring o'bells' are the eight notes of the diatonic scale: 'Do re me fa so la ti do', but the church was left with only six. The story is celebrated on the title of the local pub: The Six Bells.

But the bells – the bells. Well, maybe they bounced off the knucker's nut. Certainly he had been disturbed, because it was shortly after this that he emerged again.

Now, imagine it is medieval times.

Imagine you are down by the Knucker Hole.

Everything is still.

The air is cold.

Then the reeds start to whisper, and the water starts to move, and at the bottom of your stomach you get the dread feeling that there is something terrible, deep, deep down in the pond. A vapour rises from the surface and the water starts to bubble and boil, and bubble and boil, and something horrific starts to spiral up and up from the depths – until out of the surface of the pond appear a pair of yellow eyes. They swivel and swivel around.

They are followed by a long, green, scaly snout.

This is followed by a long, green, scaly head.

This is followed by a long, green, scaly neck.

This is followed by a long, green, scaly body, and this is followed by a long, green, scaly tail (with a pointy bit on the end, because it is well known that dragons have pointy bits on the end of their tails).

The dragon spreads its bat-like wings, and shakes the water off itself, then opens its terrible jaws, showing layers of pointy teeth, and lets out a tremendous, terrifying, heart-stopping ROAR – and out of its mouth drifts a bubble; which really is a bit of an anti-climax. The dragon has been under the water too long and the fire has gone out. The dragon mutters some obscenities to itself, opens its gob again – and ROAR. Out comes another bubble, but this one looks all misty inside, and, when it pops, there's a puff of smoke. 'I'm getting there,' mutters the dragon in medieval English, or possibly Anglo-Saxon given his age, and he opens his mouth for the third time – and we know about the number three and stories – and ROAR. This time, out of its mouth comes smoke and fire, and the dragon bellows: 'I'm back!' before flapping its wings and soaring up to Arundel Castle, where it eats seven children – and we know about the number seven and stories – before swooping back to the Knucker Hole at Lyminster.

Well, you can imagine what things were like in Arundel: there was uproar, and the people prayed that the knucker wouldn't return. But it did. The next afternoon it swooped down on Arundel and ate seven more children, before diving back into the pond.

'Call out Sir Guy,' screamed the people of Arundel, and so Sir Guy of Arundel, Lord of Arundel and all that lay under its dominion, was called forth to do battle with the mighty dragon.

'Oh dear,' he said. 'Do I have to?' You see, he was getting on in years and it was twenty years since he'd last had a battle, or rescued a princess, or a prince, or suchlike.

'Yes, you do,' quoth the people, 'get thy bloody armour on.'

The armour had gone all rusty with age and lack of use, but they oiled it up with the WD40, got him in it, and hoisted him up onto his horse with a special knight-in-armour hoisting winch. (One time, when I was telling this story, I was severely reprimanded by a serious re-enactor. 'It's nonsense about winches,' she scolded, 'knights were never winched onto their horses, that's a complete myth.' Well, this IS a bloody myth, so Sir Guy was winched onto his horse.)

They handed him his spear, and his shield emblazoned with the arms of Arundel, and Sir Guy waited outside the city gates for the return of the terrible dragon.

A dot appeared in the sky, soaring closer and closer, until the dragon loomed over Sir Guy, grinning terribly and blowing smoke rings.

'Well well, a knight in armour,' quoth the beast, 'and I do like my food in tins.'

'Have at thee, foul fiend from hell!' bellowed Sir Guy, who knew the sort of language a knight should use when confronting a dragon. 'Prepare to meet thy doom, for I shall slay thee.' He raised his shield, levelled his lance, and galloped towards the knucker. The dragon opened his mouth and ate the galloping knight, horse and all, after which he spat the armour out and ate seven more children to take the taste away.

This was a terrible time for Arundel – knights came from all over the land to do battle with the knucker, but they all got eaten, and after a while members of the knighthood began to think that discretion was the better part of valour, and they stopped coming.

In the end it was Jim Pulk who slew the dragon. He may not have been aware that it was partly his fault that the knucker had been awoken; but anyway, he resolved to slay the beast. Jim Pulk was the Lyminster baker's boy, and was a genius with the dough; he could turn out a pie or a slab of lardy cake better than anyone. Jim baked an enormous Sussex churdle pie – and if you want to know what that is you'll have to look it up, because this isn't a recipe book – and the smell of the pie was so mouth-wateringly delicious that when it drifted up to Arundel, the people temporarily forgot their misery. Then Jim went into the woods and gathered a basket full of those red toadstools with the white spots, fly agaric. They are very poisonous (they are also a hallucinogen, but that's another story), and he mashed them up with his fingers and put them in the pie. Then he picked the berries of the deadly nightshade, and he mashed them up with his fingers and put them in the pie. After this he hoisted the pie onto a big wooden cart that was pulled by six white oxen. (In folk tales carts are often pulled by six white oxen and I'm sure that there's a profound reason for this, but not being a proper folklorist I haven't the first idea what it is.) They then hauled the pie down to the Knucker Hole.

'Mr Knucker, Mr Knucker,' shouted Jim. 'Be you at home?'

The delicious smell of the pie must have penetrated even down into the depths of the pond, because deep down something started to move. Steam came from the surface, and the water started to bubble and boil, and out came the nostrils of the knucker, which after sniffing the delicious aroma of churdle pie, was rapidly followed by a long green scaly head and a long green scaly neck. The knucker looked down at Jim and the pie, and Jim looked up at the knucker.

'Oh, Mr Knucker,' proclaimed Jim, 'mighty Mr Knucker. You be such a fine and handsome beast, such a distinguished and powerful specimen of knuckerhood – and I admires thee so much, sir, that I have made thee an offering; I have baked thee the finest of Sussex churdle pies.'

'For me?' enquired the knucker.

'For you, sir,' answered Jim.

'Yum,' bellowed the knucker, and without further ado, he swallowed up the pie in one gulp. He didn't just swallow up the pie; he swallowed up the dish wot the pie was in. He didn't just swallow up the dish; he swallowed up the cart wot the dish was on. He didn't just swallow up the cart; he swallowed up the six oxen wot was pulling the cart.

'Yum,' roared the knucker again, 'yummy, yummy, yum.' But then there was a terrible churning, gurgling sound and the knucker clutched his belly, after which he lifted his right leg and fired off a fart so foul that it floored everyone between there and Littlehampton. 'Oh,' he spluttered, and keeled over, stone dead. Jim upped with his axe and chopped off the knucker's head. Up in Arundel the people shouted and cheered and rushed down to the Knucker Hole, singing the praises of Jim Pulk. They hoisted him onto their shoulders and they all went marching off to the Six Bells pub (which had until recently been known as the Eight Bells), shouting, 'Well done, Jim! Well done, Jim!'

'Well done, Jim,' beamed the landlord, 'free drinks for everyone, and the first pint for Jim Pulk.' Jim took the pint and drank – glug – glug – glug – down in one.

Then he wiped his mouth with his hand.

Oh dear me – a terrible mistake. Remember the fly agaric? Remember the deadly nightshade berries? Jim had never washed his hands. When he wiped his mouth he poisoned himself and fell down dead.

The people were inconsolable. Jim had saved them, and now he was dead. One minute they had been shouting and cheering, the next minute they were bawling and crying.

'Poor, poor Jim – he saved us all, and now he's dead.' They carried on drinking, because it was free drinks, but they laid his body out on the table and held a wake.

'Oh, poor Jim, my heart be broken; I'll have another pint please, and a packet of pork scratchings.'

The next day they took his body to the churchyard of St Mary Magdalene, Lyminster, and that's where he was buried.

Nowadays, if you go into the church, you will see a stained-glass window with a picture of a dragon. Also inside the church there is a strange old gravestone, which used to be outside, in the churchyard. The inscription got worn away by the weather and the vicissitudes of time, so most people don't know what the stone is. I know, though; it's the gravestone of Jim Pulk, and the reason I know is because that's what a bloke in the Six Bells pub told me when he told me the story – and he wouldn't lie to me, and I wouldn't lie to you.

SUSSEX ZOMBIES

Arundel Castle has seen more than its fair share of conflict over the years. Before the Civil War plunged England into chaos, Arundel Castle had already seen nearly 600 years of peace and war. Stories of the Civil War often underestimate the full horror of that time, but Arundel took its share of that horror. When the bleak New Year's Day of 1644 came to Arundel, the castle had already been besieged once and changed hands, but on 1 Jan 1644 the Royalists were in control. Within a few days, however, the Parliamentarian General Waller arrived fresh from victory at the Battle of Alton. Being a General during the Civil War required a toughness and guile beyond that required for combat; troops could swap sides at the drop of a hat, they could desert, they could mutiny – especially the fickle London regiment that Waller was in command of –

and any account of a civil war that sees things neatly in terms of two sides is inevitably a simplification of the general mess that comprises human conflict.

Waller was both tough and astute. He mounted guns in the church tower and blasted the castle walls, but worse for the inhabitants, he drained the lake that provided their water.

If you go to the old castle keep, which now sits in the middle of the Victorian extensions that have glued themselves grandiosely to the medieval heart, you can look down a deep, deep well. This well is the heart of the whole place, as wells so often are, because without water we are nothing. When that well dried up, the Royalists were driven mad with thirst.

The story is that emaciated, dehydrated, scarecrow-like figures can be seen, walking like somnambulant Sussex zombies, from the well and through the walls of the Victorian additions, out into the gardens. Should you go into the castle gardens and look into some of the obscure corners, by potting sheds and glass houses, you might see them, looking like scrawny, twisted scarecrows. Be careful; they may still be thirsty.

The Caretaker's Story

If you are visiting Arundel, and need to escape from knuckers, giants, zombies and 'stuff', you may want to take a wander up Mill Lane, by the lovely River Arun. The castle looks down at you from the left, and then gives way to Arundel Park, wherein lies poor Bevis. On your right you'll have the Arundel Wildfowl reserve; what a choice of beautiful options! A lot of people carry on up to the Black Rabbit Inn at Offham, and have a drink, something to eat, and sit and dream by the river. I'm rather fond of doing that.

Given the 'No Through Road' sign, people don't usually go any further. If you do, the road becomes a sunken lane and takes you to the rather mysterious village of South Stoke. The Arun comes meandering down through a damp and misty flood plain from Amberley Swamp – a really strange part of Sussex that you don't get to see from the road. This flat, marshy land lies in a gap in the South Downs, a gap cut by the shifting river, and is as full of Jackie Lanterns, will-o'-the-wisps, and corpse candles as any part of the Cambridgeshire Fens or the Somerset Levels. Just ask any of the night fishermen.

South Stoke doesn't have a lot in it, though it does have a lovely little church that would have been lovelier if the Victorians hadn't decided to improve it. The church is called St Leonard's, and St Leonard was another Sussex dragon slayer, but we'll meet him later. You might pass through here if you're walking the Monarch's Way, which follows the legendary escape route of King Charles II in 1651, but we'll meet him later too! If you're driving, though, you'll have to turn round and go back the way you came.

Except, apparently, when the road decides to do something really rather odd. There are hints of this in the old stories, hints of lunacy out on the marshes, hints of people, whole horses and carts disappearing. Smugglers' tales maybe? Stories, however, continue; and this is a story I heard from the caretaker of a school in Littlehampton.

He was an obliging sort of a chap, and the owner of a white van. The head teacher asked him if he'd drive up to Crawley to pick up a photocopying machine. The head teacher's husband, Roger, had retired, and he said he'd go along as well. They headed up to Arundel, undecided whether to turn left for the A284, or right for the A280, but both men being fond of meanderings and peregrinations, they decided to take the road in between – the little road that leads past the Black Rabbit. Neither of them had lived in Sussex that long, and they thought it would probably connect up to the A284 or the A29, the roads heading towards Billingshurst and thence on to Crawley. Being men, they were too busy gossiping when they passed the No Through Road sign, and carried on down a long sunken lane.

'It was weird,' the caretaker told me, 'the countryside seemed to change; it didn't look like Sussex.' The hills were higher and the ground was heathery, as if the soil was acidic, rather than chalky.

They entered South Stoke – at least they thought it was South Stoke – and then the road started to climb. The South Downs are high hills, airy and exhilarating, and the hills sometimes have names like Mount Harry, or Mount Caburn, but these hills were too high, and they were craggy and peaty, and the glistening stream way down below couldn't be the River Arun.

They entered a village as if they were in a dream, and Roger leaned out and asked a woman if this was the road to Billingshurst. She looked at him blankly.

'I dinnae ken where that is,' she said.

'Where are we?' he asked.

'You're at Spittal of Glenmuick,' she replied, 'but the road doesnae go further than this. Are ye walking to Loch Muick?'

Baffled, stunned, the two men turned the van round and headed for Ballater, before taking the long and beautiful road to Banchory, down to Brechin, and then south.

They were both in deep doo-doo when they finally got back to Sussex; the head teacher suspected them both of just deciding to wander off to the Scottish Highlands for a whisky drinking and fishing holiday, and she could hardly put the caretaker on a disciplinary, given he was with her husband.

'The strangest thing, though,' the caretaker told me, 'was that whatever happened seemed to get hold of Roger's brain, and affect his memory.' It just faded and faded.

A few weeks later the caretaker tried to talk to him about it.

'What the hell happened?' he asked.

'What are you talking about?' said Roger, 'We went to Crawley and picked up a photocopier; look, there it is.'

Well, I thought I would check the caretaker's story out; after all I'm a serious folklorist, and always rigorous with my sources. I was telling stories in the school (feeling slightly inferior to the caretaker), when Roger came in; being retired he often liked to help out with children's reading, or this and that.

I asked him about the caretaker's story.

'I really don't know what you're talking about,' he said, and so I knew. The caretaker was right; the story was true.

So he wouldn't lie to me.

And I wouldn't lie to you.

LORD MOON

South Stoke and Amberley are close to each other, both sitting on the edge of the flood plain of the River Arun, in that marshy gap in the South Downs. Our modern sense of landscape tends to be very conditioned by the linearity of roads – we see what we see from car windows – and in Sussex particularly, that means we can underestimate the wide, wild sweep of the Downs. It also means that South Stoke and Amberley seem a long way apart, as they are not directly connected by road. Yet, if the ground is dry enough, wander up by the river – they are part of the same area, both on the edge of Amberley Swamp.

Amberley has a lively past: it was both agricultural and industrial; it had chalk pits, where the very dangerous trade of lime making was carried out, and a railway line to carry the lime away. Amberley Museum & Heritage Centre carries some hints of this; and it is positioned next to the railway station. The village itself, though, is located further up the road. It is very picturesque, and the only house that is actually called 'The Thatched House' is one of the few cottages that isn't thatched.

The Revd E. Noel Staines wrote a beautiful little celebration of the village, *Dear Amberley*, in 1968. I bought a copy in the church of Saint Michael and found it to be a real labour of love. The Revd Staines begins his preface with: 'It is said that all that is needed for a village is a church, a green, and a public house. This leaves out one very important feature, namely people.' The Revd Staines writes about people and their doings with real affection, but it is sad to relate that the last time I perambulated the village, I encountered not a single soul. One of the fates of being picturesque in an age when a view is a commodity is that the real, working, everyday life seems to have been exported elsewhere.

Amberley has a castle, but I'm told that it isn't really a castle, it's a fortified manor house. But it's very old and looks like a castle, so that'll do me. It is now, however, a very posh hotel, so you can only see it from the outside. At its foot, next to the Arun flood plain, you can gaze up at the castle wall and see holes in which dwell jackdaws and doves. The jackdaws seem to dominate. You can look across the often misty-moisty flood plain, and see the six-sided Sussex steeple of Bury Church, and should you brave the Sussex clay to get to the church which looks so tantalisingly close, you'll find your way blocked by the River Arun. (Once upon a time there was a ferry.)

When the mist lies in the valley, when the jackdaws croak and the doves look nervous, when Bignor Hill, fronted by Egg Bottom Coppice, floats above the mist, it is easy to believe in mad Lord Moon. The Revd Staines mentions him, but so do the night fishermen from Littlehampton and Worthing, who take up their fishing positions on the other side of the Arun, at Bury. They can tell you about the moon face that flits around in the darkness, about the fisherman's stool being kicked away from under his ample rump, about mad laughter from across the river.

Maybe Lord Moon is ancient. Maybe he paddled up the river in one of the Iron Age dugout canoes, fragments of which have been discovered in the flood plain. Maybe, as the Revd Staines mentions, Lord Moon was the son of Captain Goble, who went bankrupt in the 1850s. When Lord Moon returned to Amberley twenty-five years later, they rang the church bells for him. Staines tells us that Lord Moon was 'remembered for his feats of running over the river, and catching hold of the sweeps of windmills while revolving, and going round with the vanes. Once in a high wind at Amberley Mill he was thrown over a 16ft high fence, but falling on newly ploughed land, it broke his fall without serious injury. Another amusement of his was running on top of quickset hedges with youth on terra firma, and beating them.'

It was surely Lord Moon who encouraged the women of Amberley to lift up their skirts in front of the fire, thus earning Amberley people the nickname of 'yellow bellies'. It must have been him behind the numerous riots and punch-ups they used to have. He must have been responsible for the fallen tree in the vicar's garden being blown back upright (though it blew down again the following week) ... and it MUST have been Lord Moon who encouraged the falling out between the vicar and the church band. John Pennicott, the clarinettist, was bandmaster. He fell out with the vicar, though only Lord Moon knows why, and the band remained silent during a church service.

'Are you going to play or not?' asked the vicar from the pulpit.

'No,' said Pennicott.

'Well then, I'm not going to preach,' said the vicar, and descended from the pulpit, something which rather begs the question as to whether or not this was a bad thing.

When the vicar walked off down the village street, the band gave him 'rough music', which is a Sussex term for following someone whilst making a terrible cacophony, done when you consider that person has in some way disgraced himself. After this the band went on strike, so the vicar 'froze the taps'; that is, he told the landlords to refuse to serve any of the band with liquor. The bandsmen got their revenge by whitewashing the vicar's windows from top to bottom, during the night.

Perhaps Lord Moon needs to liven things up, and make himself a bit more active in Amberley again. Go down to the river at night, though, and you may well see him dance. Go night fishing – if you can get a permit – and feel the madness drift in from Amberley Swamp and Bury Hollow, down the hill from Egg Bottom Coppice, or over the dykes and ditches of Amberley Wild Brooks. Wander out into those parts of Sussex that are away from the roads, get your feet wet in Sussex clay, feel the landscape and encounter stories.

There was an old woman tossed up in a basket,
Tossed high in the sky by Lord Amberley Moon.
What she did there, I couldn't but ask it,
For in her hand she carried a broom.
'Old woman, old woman, old woman,' says I,
'Oh where are you going, up so high?'
'To sweep the cobwebs from the sky,
And dance with a knucker, and eat Churdle Pie.'

3

THREE HILLS

If I was to begin this chapter by describing a pub, you might well think that because this is a book of folk tales, the pub would be an old thatched inn, and inside there would be some old gaffers, some farm workers still wearing their gaiters, a passing stranger to tell a tale, foaming tankards of ale, and a game of shove ha'penny.

The assumption, though, is that folk tales are fixed in a bucolic past. Folk tales stretch into the past, but they will also sit in the present and grope towards the future, and the pub I'm about to describe doesn't quite fit that description.

It's in a rather drab part of Worthing, and it has a large plasma TV permanently tuned to Sky Sports, seats with torn plastic covers, and men leaning on the bar befuddled by alcohol and various other substances. So, when a half-decomposed corpse shuffles in and leans on the bar with them, nobody notices. They're used to him anyway, he's quite often there, and he seems to have got hold of modern money and the ability to order a pint of lager. Every so often he calls out in a rasping voice, 'Is it doomsday yet?', but no one takes any notice; after all, he's not the only one who occasionally shouts out a random phrase.

THE MILLER OF HIGHDOWN HILL

If you follow him as he leaves the pub, you will see him shuffle through streets and cutways, along lanes at the backs of gardens – all the while with lager leaking out of various bodily perforations – out of the edge of Worthing, across the A259 (this has been known to cause problems) and up Highdown Hill. He arrives at an oblong, stone tomb, just below the Iron Age hill fort, climbs over the iron railings that surround it, stands on his head, and then slowly disappears, head first, into the tomb.

He is John Oliver, the miller of Highdown Hill. During life he ground his corn, bought and sold, and lived the social and solitary life of a miller. Social, because he was at the centre of economic life; the corn came to him from the farms and he would haggle and bargain over the price; solitary, because there he was, in his windmill:

… the fool on the hill,
Sees the sun going down,
And the eyes in his head,
See the world spinning 'round.

In his lovely *Highways and Byways in Sussex*, E.V. Lucas romantically describes the windmill standing 'high and white, a thing of life and radiance and delicate beauty, surrounded by grass, in communion with the heavens. Such noise as it has is elemental, justifiable, like a ship's cordage in a gale'.

Up on the hill, 'in communion with the heavens', John Oliver mused upon his own mortality. Whilst he was still a young man he had his coffin made, and he put it under his bed. He then had wheels fitted to the coffin, and used to get up every midnight to oil them.

Next he had a tomb built, and in an alcove near the tomb he had built a mechanical arrangement of death's heads – just in case (writes Lucas) 'as with Dr. Johnson's philosopher, cheerfulness would creep in'.

The miller lived with his coffin and his tomb for many years – he died in 1793 at the age of eighty-four. Love death – die old.

His funeral was everything a funeral should be; no bleak mourning and dressing in black. He had left word that everyone should wear merry, festive clothes, and the homily was read by a little girl of twelve:

Rejoice not against me, O mine enemy: when I fall, I shall arise; when I sit in darkness, the Lord shall be a light unto me.

I will bear the indignation of the Lord, because I have sinned against him, until he plead my cause, and execute judgment for me: he will bring me forth to the light, and I shall behold his righteousness. (Micah 7:8-9)

He had himself entombed upside-down, so that, come the day of judgement when the world was turned upside-down, he'd be the right way up …

The windmill has long gone – but the tomb is still there.

These stories attach themselves to singular places, and Highdown Hill is a singular place. These Sussex hills of chalk and flint are often singular places, but some feel more so than others. I have to confess that for me, the Trundle (mentioned in Chapter One) rather disappoints. It is a prominent hill with an Iron Age hill fort, and it should have that feeling about it, but maybe the domestication and suburbanisation of the surrounding countryside militates against that. But then, this should apply to Highdown Hill – the southern view encompasses Goring and Worthing, and it's closer to urban areas than the Trundle. For me, though, Highdown Hill has that singular magic.

The nineteenth-century tale of John Oliver has probably added itself to older legends, an occupation from the Neolithic to the Iron Age to the Romans to the Saxons and onwards must have left stories in the memory; the memories of people as well as the memory of the landscape. John Oliver did exist, and the tomb is there. The story of his upside-down burial spread throughout England, and was soon claimed by the isolated tomb of every death-obsessed eccentric. But that was John Oliver, and if he was still alive I would like to have a drink with him. I won't visit that pub and have a drink with his animated corpse though, because they don't sell any decent beer.

CISSBURY RING

North-east of Highdown Hill, we come to Cissbury Ring; another hill. Cissbury Ring is wonderful.

From here you can see the great escarpment of the South Downs marching eastward, and on a clear day you can see from Beachy Head to the Isle of Wight. The ground is rich with the wild flowers of chalk downland, and this makes it one of the best butterfly sites in the south of England. The Iron Age hill fort that creates the ring must have been a commanding sight, when its chalk ramparts gleamed white over the surrounding countryside.

At the western end of the fortress enclosure there are lumps and hummocks and holes and hillocks alive with unique downland vegetation: bee orchids, field fleawort, round-headed campion. These are the remains of Neolithic flint mines, thousands of years older than the hill fort. Around 5,000 years ago this was a major industrial site.

At that time flint was the major component of nearly all tools – whether tools for hunting, for skinning, for agriculture, or for building. Flint is mysterious. Chalk is comprised of the skeletons of trillions of ancient sea creatures, and flints are found in chalk: 'Even now geologists are unclear about precisely how it forms but it seems likely that at some point, millions of years ago, a thick, gloopy material trickled inside gaps and cavities bored into harder sediment by sea creatures like molluscs,' writes Neil Oliver in his *A History of Ancient Britain*. Sussex farmers have been said to believe that flint grows like a weed, because every time they plough, more flints come to the surface. This might damage the plough, but they've always been a good building material, and flints that have been knapped – split to expose a smooth, dark, cold, shiny surface – used to be known as Sussex diamonds.

In the Neolithic period they were vital, and the mines weren't just providing these diamonds for a local need – Cissbury was an important industrial site providing flints for trade; Cissbury flints have been found throughout Europe. The miners dug deep, and they knew what they were doing, for they dug through inferior flints to deeper seams of high-quality flints.

> The sheer physical effort involved in the extraction of mines almost beggars belief. Working primarily with picks made from red deer antlers, Neolithic miners removed thousands of tons of chalk from every shaft.

Neil Oliver writes this about Grimes Graves in Norfolk, but it is just as applicable to Cissbury Ring. 'Back in the daylight other specialists worked the raw flint into blanks for axes that were then distributed far and wide throughout the country for finishing and eventual use.' So surely Cissbury must have stayed long in the folk memory; as a place riddled with tunnels, and as a provider of a material so important it seemed magical.

After the time of flint, Cissbury maintained its importance with the building of the Iron Age fort, then the Romans moved in, and a thousand years after that it resumed its role as a place of treasure. Sometime around 1020 the Saxons moved their royal mint from nearby Steyning to Cissbury. Threats of invasion were in the air, as they would be for more than forty years till that fateful year, 1066, and it was deemed prudent to transfer the mint to the relative security of this long-proven vantage point.

Later, in Elizabethan times, Cissbury was known locally as 'Old Bury', and young lads and lassies went up there to play 'Kiss in the Ring'.

> Hey-diddle-derry,
> Let's dance in the Bury.

This was in high summer, so the resultant babies were born at Eastertide, and were known as 'Easter Infants'.

All of which leads me to a story.

Well, why wouldn't it? Tunnels, treasure, flints and folk – Cissbury has to be a hill full of tales.

The Cissbury Serpent

The story begins at Offington Hall. There was always a legend about a tunnel that connected this hall to Cissbury Ring. Throughout the land there are stories of tunnels leading from manor houses, churches or graveyards to hidden treasure – but hasn't Cissbury Ring been riddled with tunnels, and tunnel stories, for thousands of years?

Since the fourteenth century, Offington Hall had stood; a great, gaunt, building, surrounded by its own parkland. When it was demolished in 1808, a guard was kept around a particular hole in the ground, amidst the foundations.

Then a new hall was built that was even more gaunt than its predecessor, and it continued with the legend of a tunnel hidden behind oak panelling.

During Victorian times the metropolis of Worthing grew and grew until it swallowed up the parkland surrounding Offington Hall, as it swallowed up much else, including a Knucker Hole, which was near the present location of East Worthing railway station, and the culverted Teville Stream – oh the cold breaths of dreams that lurk under our layers of tarmac and concrete!

In 1963 the second Offington Hall was also demolished, and the tunnel now lies hidden amidst sewer pipes, underground streams, the supply pipes of Southern Water, fibre optic cables – and the descent of a Knucker Hole down into the bottomless reaches of a never-ending story. Just as well it's not accessible – the tunnel is terrible.

In the middle of the nineteenth century, the tenant of Offington Hall was a bit of a rake; a drinker, a gambler, and a few other things besides. Having blown his fortune at the card table, he decided to break the age-old taboo against penetrating the tunnel, and get his hands on that treasure.

Accompanied by two of his drinking, gambling companions, all carrying lanterns, they slid back the secret door and entered the tunnel.

It's a long way from Offington Hall to Cissbury Ring when you're crawling down a tunnel, and it feels even longer when that tunnel starts to twist and turn, when you're sometimes on your belly and sometimes on your back, when your lantern is stealing the oxygen you need to breathe, when you bitterly regret having entered this hellish tunnel, but there is no way you can wriggle backwards; and when the claustrophobia-induced panic makes your lungs swell, and makes the tunnel seem even tighter.

After what seemed an eternity of this crawling and wriggling, the air started to become fresher, and the tunnel started to widen and heighten; until they were walking towards a silvery light.

They entered a huge cave, and there was a great pile of silver coins: Cissbury coins. The eyes of the three men glittered as they approached the treasure, but then they saw two great feet protruding from behind the heap of silver. Slowly a great figure heaved itself to its feet; a figure that wore chain mail and an iron helmet. In place of one of its eyes was a great, weeping, bleeding wound.

'My kingdom, have you brought me back my kingdom?' roared King Harold, 'My kingdom, my kingdom.' He lurched towards the terrified men. 'You have awoken me – if you have not my kingdom, I will crush you.'

The three men flung themselves back towards the tunnel, but its entrance was just a mass of hissing serpents – or was it one serpent with many heads?

King Harold roared, the serpents hissed and spat, and desperately the men ran around the perimeter of the great circular cavern, till they reached a passage on the far side. They hurled themselves through it, and found themselves running down a long, wide tunnel – comfortable enough for them, but too small for the giant. King Harold's voice faded into the distance.

The three men had lost their lanterns, but the tunnel was illuminated by flaming torches, and then by a greeny-blue glow up ahead. Harold's voice had faded behind them, but ahead of them they heard the chip-chip-chipping, the banging and hammering of stones, which got louder and louder till they entered an enormous glowing cavern, many times larger than the cave of the one-eyed king.

The cavern was filled with a busy, buzzing host of men; all chipping, cleaving, hammering at flints. The treasure pile was a heap of glistening Sussex diamonds: knapped flints whose dark, cleaved sides shone, black, blue and green.

The eyes of the three men were drawn to the far side of the cavern where, sitting on a great stone throne, was an enormous serpent – a knucker. Behind it, the back of the throne was one enormous flint, whose smooth, cleaved surface shone with dark, shimmering colours.

As the three men, beyond fear now, gazed across the cavern, all the work stopped, the banging and hammering ceased, and the whole throng of busy workers turned and stared at them.

The head of the knucker seemed to telescope towards them.

'Ssssso,' said the knucker, who seemed at times to be male, and at times to be female, 'ssssso – you knap. Flintsses, flintsses. Ccccisssbury, Ssssussex diamonds. KNAP, KNAP, KNAP.' He, or was it she, screeched: 'KNAP, KNAP, KNAP!'

Blindly the three men turned back to the tunnel, but it hissed with the heads of serpents. All the workers around them seemed to be snakes, serpents, knuckers; till the whole floor seemed to be heaving.

The great knucker's face was above them, behind them, in front of them.

'KNAP, KNAP, KNAP,' she screamed, he screamed.

And so they did. For a long, long night they knapped flints until their muscles ached, their hands bled, and they were ready to curl up and die.

Then came a time when they realised all was silent, except for the sound of their own flint-knapping. They looked around them. No serpents – no knucker. They looked at each other, paused, and then spontaneously and simultaneously, they all fled to the passageway. They entered the smaller cavern, tip-toed around the sleeping, one-eyed king, and entered the original tunnel. There followed a long, dreadful, haunted wriggle through the pitch blackness.

Finally they reached the end, but when they did so, the noise was as bad as the cacophony in the knucker's cave. They pushed aside cracked and broken panelling, to see a half-destroyed building, and strange, blank-faced monsters battering the ruins of Offington Hall. A man shouted at them, so they stumbled off into an unknown world.

The year 1963, when the second hall was demolished, was a long time from the 1850s, but the three men had to learn how to half-adapt in their own way.

By the millennium they'd spent more of their lives in the twentieth century than they had in the nineteenth – and they seemed doomed to live long lives; still befuddled and confused by all that had happened to them.

I last came across them a few years ago in Brighton, sitting on a bench in a park, drinking Special Brew. They were swapping stories with another crazy man, who had some mad tale about being a revenue officer at Selsey. I like to hear stories from all sorts of people, but as they became more and more incoherent, I thought it best to leave.

CIRCUMAMBULATIONS AND CHANKLEBURY

Of our trio of hills (and hill forts), it is Chanctonbury Ring that has the most sinister reputation – and given that the last two stories haven't entirely been chronicles of cheeriness, that might seem surprising.

From the north, that clump of trees on the ridge always draws the eye. It overlooks the town of Steyning, and that view is an important part of the town's identity. For me, though, the most enigmatic view of Chanctonbury Ring, or Chanklebury, is from Warminghurst churchyard. From here, further from Chanklebury than Steyning, the ring is just a smudge on the horizon, but one that dominates the landscape, which makes itself the focal point of the view.

Prior to 1987 it was more noticeable, because of the ring of beech trees planted around the perimeter of the Iron Age fort by a local landowner, Charles Goring, in 1760. The Great Storm of 1987 felled most of those, and if you talk to people in Steyning, it really was quite a trauma to wake up (if they'd slept through the howling storm – I did!) and see the Chanklebury beeches gone. There was some replanting after this, though it was less than successful; and now it is planned to turn the area over to a mix of native species – not least because beech roots have a destructive effect on the archaeology. From Warminghurst, however, Chanctonbury Ring doesn't need a showy plantation – there is something about the shape of the hump on the ridge that draws the eye.

Chanklebury has always attracted stories of a less than benign nature. It has been said that it is the last dwelling place of the fairies in England, and that those few of the other folk who are left are malignant towards people, who they blame for the extinction of their race. There are stories of murders, and hangings, and suicides. There are stories of necromancers, and, to bring it all up to date, but well within the same spirit, there are stories of UFOs and alien abductions.

There is always, though, some reference to widdershins circumambulations.

A circumambulation: to travel round and round a special place – usually clockwise.

Hindus and Buddhists often circumambulate temples, or holy places in the landscape, famously Mount Kailash in Tibet. This is usually clockwise, though sometimes religions do their circling anti-clockwise: the Bönpo of Tibet circumambulate anti-clockwise, and Muslims circumambulate the Kaaba in Mecca anti-clockwise during the Hajj.

In England people 'beat the bounds', or circumambulate the boundary of a parish, and I've known some to take pleasure in circumambulating London round the M25! I'm assuming that the usual clockwise nature of circumambulation is because that reflects the movement of the planets around the sun, and the spin of the earth, and thus the cycle of the seasons; how much more important this must have been to our ancestors who lived and worked on the skin of the planet – not shut up in houses, flats and workplace buildings, with the sky a blur of reflected, artificial light.

Widdershins: to circumambulate anti-clockwise.

When this is not considered the norm, it is considered trouble. In Dharamsala, the Indian home of the Tibetan government in exile, I began to do it by mistake. Having arrived there for serendipitous reasons, so not having thought about any religious or spiritual significances, I set off for a walk down a path, foolishly unaware that it took me on an anti-clockwise perambulation around the monastery. An old Tibetan woman soon put me right on that one, if not straight, and I turned the other way feeling very chastened and chastised.

Similarly, it was always seen to be a bad thing to circle a European church widdershins. All manner of things could happen – not least the summoning up of the Devil (there are still places where this is taken seriously – I was told off in Brittany for circling a church widdershins. I don't mean to do the wrong thing – I think people just like telling me off!).

If you circle Chanctonbury Ring widdershins, at night – and depending on which story you listen to that could be one, three or seven times (there are other combinations in different stories; you may have to go naked, or walk backwards, or only do it under a full moon, or count the trees as you go) – then the Devil will appear and give you a bowl of soup. When this story is recounted in guidebooks, the writer can seldom resist the temptation to point out that it seems an awful lot of work for a bowl of soup, but who knows what the soup might signify. What was given to someone who circumambulated the hill in the Neolithic period? Or the Bronze Age? Or the Iron Age, when the hill fort was constructed? Or during the time when the Romans had a temple there? What offerings were made, what sacrifices, what horrors – or what pleasant hospitalities? After all, I have performed a clockwise circumambulation of a Hindu temple and been given a bowl of very pleasant food, conveying hospitality and appreciation of the respect shown. In Chanklebury, however, the widdershins legend runs deep – and sometimes I have a vision of an Iron Age elite of priests, getting the ordinary folk to build their monuments and earthworks, telling them to take part in the enactments of their great cosmologies, circling like the planets and the seasons; and then a weary little farmer, fed up with the lot of them and their big, clever talk, circumambulating the wrong way at night, just to stick two fingers up at his overlords!

At night, it is said to be an eerie place. I have a friend who slept up there one night, and he said that he spent the most disturbing 'off-kilter' night there: 'it was like a bad LSD trip'. Quite how he knew what that was like I don't know, but he said it, not me.

In his book *The Old Ways*, Robert Macfarlane describes a night spent on the hill whilst walking the South Downs. He describes a high-pitched cry, 'more human than avian', that came from the treetops, followed by a second cry, 'Then I realised, with a prickling in my shoulders and fingers, that the voices had split and were now coming towards me: still at treetop height, but circling round the tree ring, one clockwise and the other one anticlockwise, converging roughly on where I was lying.' Elsewhere in the book Macfarlane says it was probably owls, but so many of the tales people tell about the hill involve circling.

Some years ago I sat by a wall in Warminghurst churchyard, with Chanctonbury Ring on the skyline behind me, and told stories. I was doing it for the Churches Conservation Trust, which is trying to stop so many, ancient, disused, out-of-the-way churches from disappearing. I find that one of the privileges of being a storyteller is that people tell me stories; after I'd told a few tales, and sat in the churchyard munching sandwiches and drinking tea, a woman told me a story. I can't remember it word for word, but I remember the patterns; it is full of folkloric patterns and shapes, like a ceremony, a circumambulation, or a song. She said I could tell it, but she didn't want her name to be given.

The Jealous Husband

Near Warminghurst there was a farm, and the farmer was a young man; strong, handsome, a good worker. The farm was a big one for those days, and it was on rich, fertile soil. That meant that the farmer would be a good catch for a young woman. The local farmers tried to arrange matches with their daughters, but he showed no interest.

Now, at harvest time some of the Romani travellers would come and work on the farm, helping bring in the harvest, before moving on to the next farm.

When the traveller women were working, the farmer was unable not to notice one particular young woman; oh, her long black hair, her dark, flashing eyes, and the music of her laughter. She was the one who said things that made the other women laugh; and she was the one who always sparked off the conversation. He'd watch, and pretend he wasn't watching, and he'd wonder what they were laughing about. 'They wouldn't be laughing at me,' he thought – no, of course not.

When one harvest season was gone, and the travellers had moved on, he thought he would forget her, but she was always in his mind, and at night he longed for her to be next to him. His neighbours attempted to match him with their eligible daughters, but he was unmoved by those solid, straw-haired beauties; all he could think of was the gypsy girl.

The next harvest season he attempted to talk to her, and she had to say respectful words, because he was employing her people, but she'd always manage to deflect the conversation and move away. Then there was the young traveller man who would glare at him with dark resentment when he attempted those conversations. The farmer knew he had to enlist some help.

He knew that in faraway Amberley Swamp there dwelt an old wise woman, known as Old Nan, and it was said that she could fix anything; marriages, cattle afflicted with curses, and people afflicted with the curse. He set off, on a good solid horse, along those muddy Sussex ways, bound for Amberley Swamp.

After a day's travel he arrived at the swamp as the moon rose up into the sky. Out on the marshes there was a rickety-rackety wooden hut. His horse waded through the marsh, he tethered it to a rotten post, and knocked on the door.

'What be you wanting?' said the old woman, eyeing him suspiciously.

'I wants a spell,' said he.

'They always doos,' said she, 'go in, sit down by the fire.'

As the flames danced and made pictures, as the shadows danced around the hut, like people moving, merging, falling away from one another, he told the old woman about the traveller girl, and of how he wanted her.

'And do she want thee?' said Old Nan.

'She don't think I'm the right people,' said the farmer, 'cos she be didicais, but she ent no mumper or piker, and I wants she.'

'If she don't want you, I can't do nothing,' said the old woman. 'Thinks you I'm a bloody witch? Look at you – there'd be many a young woman glad to wed thee, and many a fine lump of a girl who'd work hard, and break thy bed.'

'I wants her!' shouted the farmer. 'I wants her dark hair and her shining eyes.'

'Pah, be off with you – you don't want she, you wants a picture.'

Eventually the farmer stormed off, cursing all the wasted time away from the farm, the long journey, and the mad old woman.

As he crossed Amberley Marsh, he realised there was someone, or something, flitting around him, and as he reached a quickset hedge on the edge of the marsh, there was someone running up and down it. Round face, moon face, shining, here now, gone now.

'You wants her, you wants her,' sang Lord Moon. 'Oh yum, yum, yum – want, want, want.'

'Get away from me,' roared the farmer, as his horse whinnied in fear.

'I can make a spell – oh I can,' laughed Lord Moon. 'Can you pay?'

'Here,' said the farmer, 'coin of the realm.'

'No I don't want that. I knows you have a Cissbury shilling – I knows, I knows. Diddle diddle derry, you picked it from the bury.'

The farmer picked the strange old Saxon coin from the waistcoat pocket where he always kept it, and handed it to Lord Moon.

'Widdershins,' said Lord Moon. 'Three times. Widdershins round the church. Call out, "I wants her", and then widdershins round old Chanklebury, seven times. Picture her in your head. Call out, "I wants her", oh, and you'll have her,' and he flitted away, giggling in a most unmanly manner.

Back home, the farmer followed the instructions. Three times widdershins round Warminghurst Church as an owl hooted and mice scurried for cover, seven times widdershins round Chanklebury as owls screeched and a vixen screamed. It wasn't hard for him to picture her in his head; hadn't he been doing that long enough anyway?

The next harvest time, when the travellers came, she only had eyes for him. Then there were whisperings, then assignations, and she was in his arms, and he in hers; then there was plotting and planning, and then there was a murderously angry young Romani man; but the farmer was strong and powerful and more than a match for anyone; and then all the travellers were being thrown off the land, and the farmer spitting after their curses, and shouting that he could get good workers anywhere.

The wedding took place in the church, and those who had to be there, were there. She was beautiful in a white dress, rather than the red wedding dress of her people, and she looked like a Spanish lady. The couple went to the farm – and they were happy.

For a while.

She had such character, such warmth, such a sense of laughter, that the local women soon came to accept her: she became the centre, the linchpin, of all their conversations. She'd go down to the village and take in the washing with the other women, and she'd say things that made the other women laugh. Sometimes he'd think that they were laughing at him, but he'd felt that before, and put it to one side.

Then he'd see her walking back to the farm from the village, and if she wasn't walking that way, he thought she was; and if the men weren't looking at her that way, he thought they were.

Finally it got too much for him and he said, 'You don't need to demean yourself going down to the village to take in the washing, I can get one of the farm workers to do that. I wants you to stay on the farm.' Now, whatever spell had been cast on her, she was still a spirited woman, so she argued against that; but she was also a dutiful wife, so in the end she had to agree.

But she had the whole farm to range around, and there was always work to be done, so that was fine … wasn't it? At the end of the month she'd sit at the head of the big, wooden kitchen table, and all the farm workers would come in for their wages, and they'd sing songs like, 'Here be a health to the mistress of the house', and she'd ask questions of people, questions that showed concern. She'd know if someone's baby was ill, or if their old mother was on her death bed, and she'd ask after them.

So that was all fine, wasn't it?

Not really. The harvest workers would come to the farm. And the harvest workers he had employed after the travellers were driven away were a rough lot, known for fighting and drinking. When she talked to them, it all got too much for the farmer.

'I don't want you yere, talking to them damn mumpers,' he said. 'I wants you to stay in the farmhouse.'

She argued with that, because she was a spirited woman, but she was also a dutiful wife, so in the end she had to agree.

Still, at the end of the month she'd hand out the bread and the cheese and the cider, and even though she was stuck in the house she seemed to know what was happening round and about, and she still asked those questions that showed concern. But one day the harvest workers crowded into that kitchen, and didn't it all get too much for the farmer.

'I don't want you yere, where everyone can see you,' he shouted. 'I wants you to stay in the bedroom.'

… and he shut her in the bedroom.

… and he took two planks of wood, and bang – bang – bang – nailed them up over the window, and there she lay in the darkness, and she faded and she died.

Then his heart broke inside him; but grief – oh dear me, that's one thing – but when it's all mixed up with guilt; well, that's another thing.

'I can't take her to Warminghurst churchyard to be buried,' he thought, 'what'll the people say?'

So, in the dead of night he took her up to old Chanklebury, and he took her body and buried it amongst the roots of Goring's beech trees, on the edge of the ring. Then he stumbled back down to the farm. Never seen to smile again. How he explained her disappearance I don't know; maybe he never talked to anyone unless he was doing business with them.

One day he was sitting at the kitchen table when there came a knock at the door, and when he opened it, there stood a tinkerman. Now this was the 1840s, and there was a terrible famine in Ireland, and people were spilling across the water to

America, Wales and England, and some of them took up the trade of the tinker.

Now, if people thought the harvest workers were a rough lot for the fighting and the drinking, they knew the tinkermen were harder and worse. It was also said that some of the tinkers were descended from the old silversmiths of Ireland, and they had a bit of the magic about them, which meant you had to be even more careful. This meant that as the tinkerman trudged Sussex from the west towards the east, he'd been offered no hospitality. People had wanted the pots and kettles, or they'd wanted theirs mended, but they never asked him to come in and share their food.

'Would you be wanting any pots or kettles, or anything mended?' said the tinkerman to the farmer.

'I don't want nothing,' said the farmer. 'I've got one pot, and that's sufficient for my needs. But you looks hungry, I 'spect you'd want something to eat and drink. Come inside, and sit thyself down at the table.'

The tinkerman was astonished, but he came in and sat down, and the farmer gave him some bread and some cheese and some cider. The tinkerman ate and the tinkerman drank.

'I've had no hospitality within miles of here,' said the tinker, 'and 'tis the greatest gift. Now, I'm a tinkerman, and my ancestors are the old silversmiths of Ireland, so I've a little bit of the magic about me. Would you have a gift you want granted? I'll see if I can give it to you.'

The farmer just laughed his bitter sort of a laugh.

'I don't want nothing that you could give I,' he said.

'Come on, now,' said the tinker, 'make your wish.'

'There's nothing I want in this world that you could give me,' said the farmer.

'This world or that world,' roared the tinker, who felt he was being challenged, 'you name it and I'll grant it.'

'There's only one thing that I want,' said the farmer in a low voice, 'and that's my dear, darling wife back.'

'God love us,' said the tinker, as the blood drained from his face, 'that'd take all the magic that I have – but I made the promise –

I made the promise.' He took his pack, stumbled off outside, and was gone down the old sunken lane.

Well, time passed and time passed, and nothing happened, so after a while the farmer forgot about it. Till one morning there came a familiar old knock at the door, and, when he opened it, there she was. If she'd been beautiful before, she was even more beautiful now. It's hard to say how, but there was a light in her eyes,

something of the other side, something of the fairiesies themselves – a regular shining fairy-spark.

'Well, this time,' thought the farmer, 'I will not let my jealousy spoil things'; and she came back into his life, and if it was wonderful before, it was even more wonderful now – and if their lovemaking had been wonderful before, now it was something beyond his Sussex imagination.

She went back down to the village to take in the washing with the other women, and once again she was at the centre of the talk and the laughter. How she explained her disappearance over that time, I don't know – maybe she said she'd been off nursing her sick mother far away by the side of a green lane.

Now maybe that should be the end of the tale …

… but it isn't.

When the farmer saw her talking and laughing with the other women, he noticed an edge to their laughter, and if he was nearby you'd swear that they really were laughing at him. And when she walked back to the farm from the village; well, if the men didn't look at her before, they did now. Something about the way she walked – oh Lord, the swaying of hips, and the flash of ankle.

It all got too much for him.

'I don't want you going down the village no more!' he shouted. 'I wants you to stay on the farm.'

'If that's what you want, my darling husband, that's just what you shall have,' said she.

And so she stayed on the farm.

Then one day the harvest workers were there, and, oh dear me, didn't she flirt with the harvest workers, and oh dear me, didn't that get too much for him.

'I don't want you flaunting yourself around the farm!' he shouted. 'I wants you to stay in the farmhouse.'

'If that's what you want, my darling husband, that's just what you shall have,' said she.

And so it was: she stayed in the farmhouse, and at the end of the month she still handed out the bread and the cheese and the cider, and she still asked questions that showed she knew what was happening round and about. But now, they weren't questions that showed concern. They were questions that made people wriggle in their seats; that made them think maybe she knew things they'd rather she didn't.

Then one time the harvest workers were there, and oh dear me, didn't she flirt with the dirty shower of mumpers, and, oh Lord, didn't that get too much for him, and he hissed at her, 'I don't want you yere where every man jack can see you, I wants you to stay in the bedroom,' and he locked her in the bedroom, and he bang – bang – banged the planks up over the window.

And then, when the kitchen was empty, he thought, 'Oh dear God, what have I done?' and he opened the door, and stumbled into the darkness of the bedroom.

'I'm sorry, I'm sorry, but you're my wife, my darling wife, my beautiful wife; I can't stand them men looking at you.'

She was lying on the bed, and the sheet was pulled over her face. He stooped over her and pulled the sheet back, and a terrible stench assailed his nostrils. As his eyes adjusted to the darkness, and he stared down, what did he see but green, rotting flesh, all wriggling and heaving with maggots and worms. Her eyes snapped open, and they shone in the darkness like pale yellow lanterns. Slowly she sat up.

'Come yere, my darling husband,' said she with a voice like the scraping of stones, 'come to I, my darling husband.' He opened his mouth to scream, but nothing came out. He staggered backwards to the door as she lurched towards him, arms outstretched. 'Come yere my darling husband, come yere my love, come to I.'

Desperately he felt against the door for the door handle, but all he could feel was stone, and rock, and flints, and soil, and entwining roots.

So it was, in 1987, after all those trees had blown down on poor old Chanklebury, that people found, entwined in and penetrated by tree roots that had ripped up out of the ground, two skeletons – one of a man, and the other of a woman; and though they were shattered by the roots, you could still see that the arms of the woman were wrapped around the man. When the archaeologists tested them, to see if it was all part of some ancient burial rite, they found that they only dated back to the first half of the nineteenth century, after Goring had planted those beech trees.

The woman who told me the story said that the strangest thing, though, was the skull of the man. You can't tell an expression from a skull, because an expression is made from skin, and flesh, muscles and tendons. But you'd swear – something to do with the drop of the jaw – you'd swear that when he died, he was screaming.

VALLEYS AND ALLEYS, BOTTOMS AND BRIGHTON

Place names have histories, and have passed from mouth to mouth like folk tales. In an area of only a couple of square miles, just north of Brighton, there are so many Bottoms, that to list them, with some of those other glorious non-Bottom names thrown in, we have either a poem or a story. It travels a route from the romantic and celestial Moon's Bottom, to the earthy and exceedingly smelly Hogtrough Bottom. It has to be called:

MOON'S BOTTOM

Moon's Bottom, Big Bottom,
Plumpton Plain,
Derchen Bottom, Shambledean Bottom,
Balmer Huff,
North Bottom, Home Bottom,
Middleton Bostail,
Stump Bottom, Long Bottom,
Granny's Belt,

Falmer Bottom, Landport Bottom,
Swanborough Hill,
Cuckoo Bottom, Loose Bottom,
Buckland Hole,
Faulkner's Bottom, Hogtrough Bottom,
Scabby Brow.

Oh, the irresistible deliciousness of place names. And where there is a bottom there has to be a top, and the tops are ups, and the ups are the Downs. Yet, Brighton is in some ways strangely disconnected from the South Downs that loom over it. Brighton seems more connected to London; both by the railway and by the much driven, cycled, jogged, charity-run A23. But just five miles north of Brighton there is a wondrous place: the longest, deepest and widest 'dry valley' in the UK – the Devil's Dyke.

In 1860, William Harrison Ainsworth published *Ovingdean Grange*, a romantic novel set during the Civil War. It has to be said that as a work of literature *Ovingdean Grange* hasn't really passed the test of time, but Ainsworth clearly knew and loved Sussex, and his landscape descriptions are lovingly detailed. He describes the Devil's Dyke as a 'remarkable chasm'.

> The precipitous escarpment, which stands like a ... beautiful tract being discernible at one glance from it – slopes suddenly and abruptly down, without the slightest interruption to the valley, the perilous nature of the descent being materially increased by the slippery condition of the turf, which offers, at dry seasons especially, a very insecure footing ...

This description occurs as a Cavalier is being pursued over the edge of the Devil's Dyke by Roundheads. After this, Ainsworth, for no apparent reason, drops out of his story, and for one whole chapter, a schoolmaster called Cisbury Oldfirle recounts 'The Legend of the Devil's Dyke'. This chapter proved popular, particularly to the Victorian and Edwardian tourist industry, and was frequently reprinted as a booklet in its own right. I enjoy it very much, but this is the real version:

The Legend of the Devil's Dyke

Satan came to earth.

God threw the rebellious angel out of heaven and he tumbled and tumbled through the firmament until he landed with a crash in Sussex. He lay there for a while, gazing at the sky and scratching his private parts, whilst around him Christianity arrived in Sussex with the last of the Romans. Satan sneezed, farted, and with the coming of the Saxons, Christianity was blown away again. Whilst most of England became Christian, Sussex remained pagan. Sussex was an isolated county – something that seems strange now that those metalled roads have brought it within the sphere of London, and caused much of the county to feel suburbanised.

Then St Wilfrid brought Christianity back to the county. He used his own methods, which involved a great deal of violence; Christianity being good at ignoring the teachings of Christ. Churches started to appear all over the Weald and the tolling of church bells began to penetrate Old Nick's reverie. He raised his horned head, saw all the churches, let out a dreadful oath against God, shouted: 'Is there no rest for the wicked?', glared around him, saw the blue sea shining beyond the fishing village of Brighthelmstone, and roared, 'That's it, I'll drown the lot of you, I swear to God – him up there – I will. I'll dig a dyke and let in the sea, and if I'm not done by the morning I swear I'll go to hell and stay there.'

The Devil was handy with a shovel – one of the reasons for his rebellion against the Almighty was God's insistence on mechanising heavenly agriculture – and so he set to work with a will, digging a ditch to the sea.

Now at that time, Old Nan the wise woman, who later resided in Amberley Swamp, lived in a rickety-rackety wooden hut on the edge of Rag Bottom Copse. As the Devil worked with a will, flinging clods of earth in all directions, panic-stricken hermits and would-be-saints hammered on the old woman's door, imploring her for help. She muttered and grumbled and half-thought that silencing those bloody bells wouldn't be such a bad idea, but realising that her rickety-rackety wooden hut would be swept away with everything else, thought she'd better foil Old Gooseberry's plans.

'Crow, Chanticleer,' she said to the cockerel, which was her most ungodly familiar.

'Cock a doodle doo,' said the cockerel, without enthusiasm.

'Bloody crow, or you're in the pot,' she snapped.

'COCK A DOODLE DOO,' crowed the cock.

'What's that?' said Satan. 'This can't be. 'Tisn't near morning.'

'COCK A DOODLE BLOODY DOO,' crowed the cock again.

'NO, NO,' roared the Devil, and dug faster.

Old Nan then lit a candle, held it behind a sieve, and raised it up over Mount Harry.

'Oh bloody bugger and bum,' wailed the Devil, who really ought to have had his mouth washed out with soap and water. 'Sunrise, sunrise; it can't be. To hell with me – to hell,' and he fled westwards, away from the rising sun.

So now the trench the Devil dug is the Devil's Dyke, the clods of earth are Chanctonbury Hill, Cissbury Hill, Rackham Hill, Mount Caburn and the Isle of Wight, and the churches are still dotted all over the Weald. As for the Devil, he didn't stop running until he came to Bognor – and he's remained there ever since.

Worms and maggots,
Bluebottle flies,
Buzzing around,
Old Gooseberries pies.
I've told my story,
And I've told no lies.

The King of the High Downs

In 1950 Norman Wymer wrote: 'Three or four decades ago the Downs were thick with sheep, and their bleating and the distant tinkling of their bells, together with the barking of the dogs that watched over them as they nibbled the herbage, or clustered

around a dewpond to drink, made pleasant and familiar music.'
Wymer went on to write:

> The shepherds wore high leather gaiters, slate-coloured smock frocks
> – beautifully smocked by their nimble-needled womenfolk – and
> 'chummy' hats, not unlike those worn by the old time parsons. When
> the weather appeared threatening they usually carried a large umbrella
> on their backs, and always they had their crook, which, very often,
> had been handed down by their forefathers as a family heirloom.

(Pyecombe, near the Devil's Dyke, was known for the manufacture
of a particularly local pattern of shepherd's crook, the 'Pyecombe
Hook'.) These shepherds were singular, otherworldly and
independent characters, and could look quite forbidding. In 1937
Arthur Mee wrote:

> One of the pictures that lives in the memory and will not go is the
> shepherd with his crook and his faithful dog, like Abraham with his
> flock. We saw one with hundreds of sheep, and he passed us look-
> ing neither right nor left, for he had nothing to do with the world;
> he was part of the life of the Downs as his father had been, and his
> father's father before him.

And if we go back to the seventeenth century, one such gaunt
figure could be seen, high on the Downs, surrounded by his flock.

He was a learned man, who, in the solitude of his occupation,
had taught himself to read and write with the aid of the King James
Bible, so recently translated into English, and which could be read
aloud with a rhythm that reflected the rolling of the hills. This was a
valuable possession, and he kept it hidden in a buried wooden box.

As he stood on the Down, surveying the roll of the hill towards
Pyecombe, he noticed a straggle of horses and riders snaking up the
hill, down into the valley, and then back up again. He watched them
impassively, without fear, and leaned on his crook as they approached.

They reined in their horses in front of him, and gazed at the
imposing figure of the shepherd. They were dressed as Roundhead

troopers, but their hands were too soft, particularly those of the tall, dark, central horseman – and there was something supercilious about their manner.

'Well, sir,' said the tall horseman, 'you must be a great king of all you survey.'

'Some would have it so, sir,' replied the shepherd.

The horseman laughed, but something had punctured his affected amusement.

'And what of your queen, sir?' asked the horseman.

'I have no wife, sir,' said the shepherd, ''tis just I and the high downs that you would call my kingdom.'

'Then you have no issue, no dynasty. That is a poor thing for a king.'

'I am content, sir, and there is a young man to whom I teach my skills.'

'Aha,' said the horseman, 'but he is not your son – so 'tis the end of your line.'

'Nay, sir – my line is in my skills, and they are passed on by those who work on this land; those who would create rather than destroy.'

'Aye, sir, there is much destruction in this land. So, if your dynasty means nothing to you, then you are a republican.'

'But sir, you said I was a king.'

'Ha, well answered,' replied the horseman, who had abandoned his show of superior amusement.

'I have been a king here, sir, since the last days of Queen Bess, and I have known king follow queen in faraway London, but the larks still sing high above the Downs.'

The horseman pondered on whether to be offended, for he was aware, now, that the shepherd knew who he was.

'Would you betray a king?'

'I would not, sir.'

'No, I think you would not,' said the horseman, eyeing Colonel Gunter and signalling him to take his hand away from his sword hilt.

'I wish you God speed, sir,' said the shepherd, though with a dignified demeanour, no unctuousness or servile eagerness.

'… and if 'twas the regicide Cromwell, would you wish him God speed too?'

'I would, sir,' replied the shepherd, holding his crook for all the world like a mace or a sceptre.

Charles and his Royalist faithful rode on to Shoreham and a boat bound for France. As the boat slipped out of the harbour in the dead of night, Charles' mind was chastened by a meeting of kings in a place without pomp or ceremony. The lesson probably faded, though.

TREVOR'S BOOTS

Charles II was defeated at the Battle of Worcester in 1651, and his long escape route from Worcester to a boat sailing to France from Shoreham-by-Sea is followed by a long-distance footpath called the Monarch's Way. The route of this path through Sussex, from Stansted Park to Shoreham, is much recommended, because it passes through such a variation of scenery: from parkland to Kingley Vale, to the edge of the Amberley marshes up to the high downs, and down to the sea. To walk that route, assuming you are not being pursued by Roundheads, is like walking across heaven.

The route has created its own, current, folklore. The Monarch's Way was founded by Trevor Antill, who, sadly, died unexpectedly in 2010. Trevor is a legend amongst ramblers, and at the time of writing, his boots are being carried by relay along the whole footpath, from Worcester to Shoreham. The route meanders down from the Midlands to Charmouth in Dorset, back up through Somerset, before heading west to Hampshire and Sussex; 615 miles in all. Trevor's boots: this is folklore in the making.

THE MAGNIFICENT CITY ON THE MARGIN OF THE SEA

William Harrison Ainsworth's book *Ovingdean Grange* was based around the story of Charles' escape to Shoreham, and the Downs above Brighton play an important role in the story. During the time in which the novel is set, there was no Brighton – just a fishing village called Brighthelmstone – but Ainsworth is so enthusiastic about the wonders of Brighton that he has to rhapsodise about the town of 1860, and his novel becomes, for a while, like something written by John Fowles – two time periods referring to each other:

Little did Charles II foresee, when halting on the evening in question with his escort on the smooth and pleasant slopes of the hill now laid out as Queen's Park, that on the site of the obscure fishing village towards which he gazed, would arise, some two centuries later, one of the fairest and most magnificent cities ever built upon the margin of the sea, since the time when Pompeii the Beautiful was destroyed by the fiery ashes of Vesuvius.

Significantly, Ainsworth notes the connection Brighton now has with London, rather than its Sussex hinterland:

Little did he foresee that, in the lapse of time, this remote and almost unknown fishing village on the Sussex coast should become, by agencies of which he could not dream, and which, if described, he might not have credited, so connected with the great metropolis itself, as to form almost its marine suburb.

Ainsworth is full of the Victorian confidence that can rhapsodise about the Regency Spa-cum-Victorian wonder city, but come the twentieth century, Brighton seemed to attract stories that highlighted the seamy side of things. This may be partly because of Graham Greene and his novel *Brighton Rock*, and may be partly because of the 'kiss 'n tell' effect of being a seaside town, where inhibitions are put aside for the holidays. However, every city has its seamy side, and its violence and crime, so it's probably unfair to view Brighton solely through such a prism. Indeed, a drive along the seafront, along Marine Drive towards Rottingdean, will show you how splendid it all still is. It does, however, have to be admitted that all of Brighton isn't quite so splendid. One such rather less-than-splendid place is Quadrophenia Alley, which is a place named after a story rather than a story that exists because of a place.

QUADROPHENIA ALLEY

The story is a film, and the film is *Quadrophenia*, a tale of mods and rockers battling it out on Brighton's seafront. The newspapers in the 1960s were full of apocalyptic tales of societal breakdown during this period of gang fighting; though English history is full of periodic youthful riotous behaviour, and we may observe that it didn't stop in the 1960s. In a way, the mods and rockers have become part of Brighton's folklore, and a recent film version of *Brighton Rock* confirmed this by replacing the 1930s setting with the 1960s, and featuring mods and rockers indulging in a pitched battle. *Quadrophenia*, however, created folklore by featuring a scene where the central character, London mod Jimmy Cooper, played by Phil Daniels, has a knee-trembler up an alley with Steph, played by Leslie Ash. The merging of the real and the imagined is a feature of folklore, and the alley where this was filmed has become the focus of a strange sort of pilgrimage; people come from all over the world to add their graffiti to the walls. If you want to pay a visit (though I hasten to point out that I'm not encouraging anyone to breach the peace by either indulging in knee-tremblers or spraying graffiti) then walk along Prince Albert Street (Prince Albert would never have approved, though George the Prince Regent, for whom Brighton Pavilion was built, wouldn't have turned a hair), turn right into Little East Street, look for a nineteenth-century cottage with walls made from tarred beach pebbles, then turn left down an unmarked alley marked 'To East Street'. You're there, that's Quadrophenia Alley – but it wasn't before the film.

THE BRIGHTON THING

Oh well, I was trying to criticise the habit of always referring to the seamy side of Brighton, and what story should emerge? One about knee-tremblers in alleyways! I'm afraid it's going to get worse. There are stories that you won't find in books, but which folk do tell. The idea of folk stories tends to conjure up a picture of old grannies telling tales by the fireside in country cottages, but nightclub bouncers and bar staff tell each other stories; though not in a 'once upon a time' sort of a way. You will find this story in a book now, though, because I'm about to put it there.

The crowds of people 'going clubbing' queue up outside the door and sometimes the bouncers remove various illegal substances from the punters, and these substances are then stashed behind the bar. (I did hear a rumour concerning to whom these substances were passed on, but I certainly wouldn't repeat it, because I'm sure it's untrue.)

In the early hours of the morning in one particular club, after the last sweaty body had gone, the rats appeared. Oh – nibble-nibble-nibble. Then there was a drip-drip-drip. Outside, in a bleak Brighton dawn, the rain was pouring down. The club had a tile missing on the roof, the water dripped down through a damp, rotting, stalactite of Artex, and drip-drip-dripped onto the stash behind the bar. Nibble-nibble-nibble went the rats. Plastic was punctured, rainwater mixed the substances, a rat lost its ratty little mind, a rat started to eat a rat, substances dissolved and blended – squeak-squeak-squeak – and something horrible dragged itself upright from behind the bar. SQUEAK-SQUEAK-SQUEAK. A great rat's head – or was it a horse's head – after all, isn't ketamine used for doping horses? The thing slodged out of the nightclub, heaving open the door, and then splat, squish, squelched through the early morning streets, down to the seafront. Splodge-splodge-splodge; a terrible thing lurching through the rain. Out to the pier – out along the pier – right to the end – and then SPLASH: into the sea.

Now, every so often, fat, toxic lumps are washed up along the coast; from just west of Brighton down to Selsey Bill – I've seen them myself at Bognor. Most people don't know what they are; but then concerned environmentalists don't always think of asking the opinions of nightclub bouncers.

THE FLYING DUTCHMAN OF MOULSECOOMB

The *Flying Dutchman* is famous: the legendary ship that is doomed to sail the seas forevermore, never making land; that is unless Captain Vanderdecken hands the belaying pin to another mariner, so that another ship will be doomed never to make land, only to be occasionally spotted beating through a storm off the Cape of Good Hope. Brighton has its equivalent.

Should you be driving down the A270 into Brighton, you might want to turn around again and go back up. This may be because you didn't particularly want to turn down that road; it may be that you were trying to find a way off the A27, that major road that bypasses Brighton, so you could go past the Pudding Bag, into Stanmer Park. The major road, though, just wants to hurl you into another major road before you can blink, look, and swear at the car that's tailgating you. You may think that you can just turn left off the A270, and shortcut back up again. Mistake. You are in Moulsecoomb Estate, and you will be lucky if you ever get out again. Round and round you will go – ah, here's a railway bridge; if I go under it I'm out – no you're not, you're back to the railway bridge. Staplefield Drive will take me somewhere. No, it won't – you're back again. I drove past here twenty minutes ago. Round and round you'll go – and if you are very lucky you might eventually be able to exit by the same way you went in. There is, however, a Suzuki Swift that still drives around and around, never to escape. Who knows what terrible blasphemy the unfortunate driver uttered against the deities of the highways and byways, but he's doomed to drive the Moulsecoomb Estate forevermore; that is unless he can pass on the mantle – probably a broken satnav – to another unfortunate motorist. So if anyone asks you directions in the bewildering array of streets that lie between the A270 and Hogtrough Bottom (the site of a wondrous graveyard of stolen and 'joy-ridden' cars), run, drive away, flee – or you'll be the next Flying Dutchman of Moulsecoomb.

THE SPECTRE OF DALE HILL

Those deities of the highways and byways; maybe they look after the A23. The London–Brighton road. Mods and rockers. Dirty weekends. Family cars laden with buckets and spades and fractious children. Now, the charity runs; the bicycles, vintage cars; the homemade machines.

This odd procession is English folklore, presumably starting with those Regency upper classes heading for Brighthelmstone to take the waters.

The ghost, however, must have joined the procession during the Second World War, because it's an army lorry full of wan-faced young soldiers, though their faces are always indistinct. Many a vehicle has overtaken the lorry on Dale Hill, and the driver and passengers wonder what it's doing, as they also wonder about the temporary sense of gloom and depression that besets them as

they overtake. Then they look in the rear view mirror, and there's nothing there.

Would there be a reason why troops were going to Brighton? Were they going to leave the road somewhere and head for an army camp or an embarkation point? This story is untold; we just have the story of the apparition, told since the late 1940s.

The most notable occasion, surely one that should have been mentioned in *Quadrophenia*, was when a host of mods on their elaborately decorated scooters came upon the lorry, and while they were shouting and trying to attract the attention of the faceless soldiers, it was no longer there. It didn't disappear in a flash; it was as if they thought they could see it, and then they couldn't.

Later they had all the excitement of their battling at Brighton, and the vain glorious feeling of gaining notoriety in the newspapers – and yet, many years later, some of these no-longer youngsters would be sitting and talking in a London pub, and the conversation would drift from their romanticising of the time when they went to Brighton to be a pain in the backside, and mention would be made of that old military lorry that they all thought they saw – and then they didn't.

The Signalman

There are more ghosts on the route in and out of Brighton, and why wouldn't there be? High up above Brighton, near Pyecombe, beneath the Jack and Jill windmills that stand in that freedom of sunlight and downland space, you might hear terrible cries coming from beneath the ground, and the sound of rending metal. It comes from the Clayton railway tunnel. The entrance to the tunnel is a castle; a castellated folly. The farmer who owned the land when the tunnel was built in the 1840s wouldn't allow access unless the tunnel entrance was disguised, and it was done in true Brighton style.

At the southern end of the tunnel there was a signal box, and a signalman. In the signal box there was an alarm bell linked to a signal, a needle telegraph, and a clock. The signalman,

Henry Killick, could control the signal by using a wheel; the signal would normally be at 'danger' until he allowed a train to enter the tunnel. When the train passed, the signal would return to 'danger'. If it didn't, an alarm bell would ring. The southern signal box was linked to a northern one by telegraph.

On 25 August 1861 the *Portsmouth Excursion* left Brighton station at 8.28 a.m. Just three minutes later, at 8.31 a.m., there was a hissing of steam, and the *Brighton Excursion* pulled out of the station. Then, just four minutes later, the *Brighton Ordinary* left. They were too close; Signalman Killick tried to stop the second train entering the tunnel before the first had left, so he waved his red flag. He thought the driver hadn't seen it, but actually the driver had, and had stopped his train in the tunnel. Signalman Brown, in the north signal box, then telegraphed Killick to tell him the first train had left the tunnel, but, oh Lord, Killick thought he meant the second train; so he gave the all clear to the final train, the *Brighton Ordinary*, which accelerated into the tunnel. And inside the tunnel? The second train was reversing, to find out what the problem was. Driver Gregory of the *Brighton Ordinary* saw the lights and acted with great speed, slamming his locomotive into reverse, but it was too late. The *Brighton Ordinary* obliterated the guard's van of the reversing train, and rode up over the last carriage, before being brought to a halt when its chimney stack smashed into the tunnel roof. This was the worst railway disaster ever at the time; 176 passengers were injured and twenty-three killed, most of the deaths being in that last carriage, where passengers were burned or scalded to death by the steam.

And so, those cries are still heard from beneath the ground, when up on the Downs all seems light and airy.

And the life of a signalman? Down in the gloom of the cutting, solitary and sunless, with the ever-present damp, dark, gaping mouth of the tunnel … and the responsibility; the responsibility for all those lives that would flash past in a clatter of steam and sudden light. Charles Dickens certainly thought about it, because it was this disaster, along with his own experience of being in a railway crash in Kent, that inspired his wonderful, ghostly short story 'The Signalman'.

When the night is dark and stormy,
And the clouds are black o'erhead,
When the screech-birds cry in chorus,
As if mourning for the dead,
When the wild winds are roaring,
And the air is thick with rain.
Then on such a night, with a shriek of affright,
Is seen the phantom train.

From 'The Phantom Train', by Alphonse Courlander (1881-1914), turning out a good old recitable poem, in the days of rhythm and rhyme (something that had to be reintroduced from the street, via rap!).

THE PIG IN A POKE

Seeing as we're back up on the Downs, we might as well meet the Pharisees again. This time it's not along a Pook's Lane, but up on the South Downs Way at Beeding Hill.

Once upon a time there were two disreputable Fulking farmers, who had nicked a Beeding pig, and had fled down the Bostal to Beeding Hill. As they mounted the hill, carrying the big, fat pig in a pokeputte, they felt hot and sweaty, and so they stopped to rest, putting the pig in a poke, unintentionally down on top of a Pharisee's hole. Now, the Pharisees don't like having pokes on their holes, so they were sure to pay the two Fulkingers back. After the two men had set out again, the man whose turn it was to carry the pig in a poke saw a tiny little figure running by his side.

'Dick, Dick, where be goon? Mother don't want to lose oor Dick.' From inside the poke there came the reply:

In a sack,
Pick-a-back,
Riding up Beeding Hill.

The two Fulkingers flung down the poke and fled back to Fulking, whilst piggy struggled out of the sack and piggy wiggied it all the way back to his sty. Needless to say, the farmer from whom the pig had been stolen had always been respectful towards the Pharisees, and left them out a little tin mug of milk every evening.

Trotters and bacon
Dumpling Stew
I've told my story,
And told it to you.
Beer and cider,
Nettle wine and tea,
Next time I visits,
Tell a story to me.

PUCK AND THE CARTER

Whilst we're talking about the Pharisees, I must mention the Revd W.D. Parish's truly wonderful *Dictionary of the Sussex Dialect and Collection of Provincialisms in use in the County of Sussex*, originally published in 1875. He is a vicar, so he would rather call them farisees. 'By an unfortunate use of the reduplicated plural, the Sussex country people confuse the ideas of fairies and Pharisees in a most hopeless manner,' he writes, maybe thinking of sermons gone wrong when he tried to quote from the Old Testament about the conflict between the Pharisees and the Sadducees, and his congregation were picturing a battle in the meadow between happy fairies and sad fairies. He writes: 'A Sussex man was once asked, "What is a pharisee?" and answered, with much deliberation and confidence, "A little creature rather bigger than a squirrel, and not quite so large as a fox," and I believe he expressed a general opinion.' But then the Revd Parish decided that this must be about ferrets, because, 'Since writing the above, I find that polecats are called varies in Devonshire; so that possibly the person who gave this answer had been brought in contact with some west-country folk and had the word from them. It is not Sussex.' So there.

Well ferrets, varies, fairisees, or Pharisees; the Revd Parish, under the dictionary heading: 'Farisees (Fairieses.) Fairies', recounts a wondrous story about them. He tells us, 'the following was most seriously told me', and I really think I can only relate the story as he does:

> I've heard my feather say, that when he lived over the hill, there was a carter that worked on the farm along wid him, and no one couldn't think how t'was that this here man's horses looked so much better than what anyone else's did. I've heard my feather say that they was that fat that they couldn't scarcely get about; and this here carter he was just as much puzzled as what the rest was, so cardinley he laid hisself up in the staable one night, to see if he could find the meaning an't.
>
> And he hadn't been there very long, before these here liddle farisees they crep in at the sink hole; in they crep; one after another; liddle tiny bits of chaps they was, and each an 'em had a liddle sack of corn on his back, as much as ever he could carry. Well! in they crep, on they gets, up they clims, and there they was, just as busy feeding these here horses; and prensley one says t'oth'r, he says, 'Puck.' Says he, 'I twets, do you twet?' And thereupon, this here carter he jumps up and says, 'Dannel ye,' he says, 'I'll make ye twet afore I've done wud ye!' But afore he could get anigh 'em they was all gone, every one an 'em.
>
> And I've heard my feather say, that from that day forard this here carter's horses fell away, till they got that thin and poor he couldn't bear to be seen along wid 'em, so he took and went away, for he couldn't abear to see hisself no longer; and nobody ain't seen him since.

MOUNT CABURN'S REVENGE

The Pharisees, though, have found their way into more recent stories; for don't believe that they've flitted all away – they're just harder to see.

Close to Brighton, yet far from Brighton, because we are away from that Brighton–London axis, there are villages where people would once play music. Up until the 1970s you might get a gathering of the old boys, and, more occasionally, the old girls, playing music and singing in a pub. I don't mean something self-consciously called a folk club, though some of the participants were definitely tradition bearers. (I remember seeing folk song collectors, complete with tape recorders, walk out in disgust when one man played his squeezebox, whilst a woman sang Engelbert Humperdinck's 'The Last Waltz'. They said it wasn't traditional!) The men wore hats and suits with wide lapels, and watch chains, and they played concertinas, accordions, and mouth organs. I have no recordings of this, just memories, but I am reminded strongly of it by two tracks from Shirley Collins' lovely CD *Adieu to Old England*; the tracks are: 'Portsmouth' and 'Come All You Little Streamers'. These individuals are all dead and buried now, but there was one mouth organ player from between the wars who was supposed to have been the greatest, and that was Charlie Winnick.

It was said that Charlie had been taught by the Pharisees, and I don't see why the Pharisees shouldn't have taken up the mouth organ, same as people, for it's a very transportable instrument, and the Pharisees have always been fond of making their own music.

When Charlie was a boy, he could only ever play one tune – and it was a tuneless one at that, and folk would hold their ears and shout at him. He called it 'Mount Caburn's Revenge', though no one quite knew why. Mount Caburn is a Sussex hill, though it sounds like a mountain from a fantasy land. Who needs fantasy lands, though, when we have the Sussex Downs? 'Revenge' the tune may have been – on people's ears anyway – though for what crime this vengeance was being wreaked, nobody knew.

One day, walking home from school, the other boys taunted him, took his mouth organ, and threw it over a hedge, into a field. Blinded by the tears, Charlie fumbled through the grass until he found it, and then walked miserably down the lane, till he came to a bridge over a stream, next to a turnip field.

He sat disconsolately on the parapet of the bridge and proceeded to torment his mouth organ. In the turnip field there was a scarecrow, arms outstretched. I don't know why, for what crow could carry a turnip away? Charlie could swear that it had moved. He looked again – one arm was pointing upwards – again – both arms were stretched outwards. Charlie shoved his mouth organ into his pocket and prepared to run, but in a flash – like a bad dream – the scarecrow was sitting on the parapet next to him.

'Get on my back,' said the turnip face. Wildly the boy shook his head, but the scarecrow clasped him in its raggedy arms and proceeded to hurtle up into the sky, like a rocket. It then levelled off, and, with Charlie sitting on its back, the scarecrow flew over the Sussex countryside. Charlie looked down and saw fields and farms and copses and woods and villages and rivers and streams, and in the distance, the shining sea. Ahead of them was Mount Caburn.

The scarecrow circled the hill three times, and then a door opened in the side of the hill. In flew boy and scarecrow, to be greeted by a whole host of the Pharisees – and there was a Pharisee who was 2ft tall, a veritable giant amongst Pharisees, and he had a big belly, and was wearing doublet and hose.

'Sit down here, boy,' he roared in an amiable tone, and patted a chair. Charlie sat down, and a Pharisee brought him a glass of the most delicious ginger beer. The king of the Pharisees beamed, and said, 'Go on boy, play us a tune on your mouth organ,' and Charlie did. The music he played was wonderful. He played 'Come All You Little Streamers' and 'The Sussex Whistling Song' and 'Twankydillo', and the Pharisees started to dance, and they danced, and leaped, and capered round the floor, on the benches, on the tables, round and round the walls, and over the ceiling – until Charlie was dizzy with the sight of them.

In between times he drank ginger beer and cocoa, though not mixed together, and ate chocolate and bacon sandwiches (again, not mixed together) – and he thought he was in heaven. This went on all through the night, and then it was morning and the church bells of Lewes were ringing out, and the king of the Pharisees said, 'Go on boy, get on old Mawkin's back, and he'll carry thee home,' and so he did and so he did.

There was the boy sitting on the parapet of the bridge, and there was the scarecrow, standing in the field, arms outstretched … and there was Charlie's mother, crying and shouting. 'We've all been out searching and, oh Lord, I've been at my wit's end'… and the whole village had been searching, and the bullies had been soundly walloped – and they deserved it.

When Charlie told them he'd been riding on the back of a mawkin, and he'd been inside Mount Caburn with the Pharisees, and they'd been making merry all night, they all thought he'd gone mad. But when he played his mouth organ; well, they all had to wonder.

And this is how Charlie Winnick became the best harmonica player in all of Sussex – and why he was never short of a free beer.

COME ALL YOU LITTLE STREAMERS

And so we come to 'Come All You Little Streamers'. It is a strange song; it was collected from Ned Spooner of Midhurst, and printed in the *Journal of the Folk-Song Society* in 1913. Now the area around Midhurst is in another chapter, but the song fits in this chapter. It has been suggested that the song has some sort of religious, mystical allegory in its background, but I really wouldn't know, because I haven't the first idea what it means, nor do I have the first idea why people want to know what things mean. What I do know is the pictures it conjures up, and that is one reason why it belongs in this chapter, the other being that Charlie Winnick played it inside Mount Caburn.

I can see the high downs, and wild flowers, and shining flints. Then I can see down to the sparkling sea, where ships are riding at anchor, their pennants streaming in the wind; the land and the sea, and the chalky coast of Sussex where the two come together.

Oh, come all you little streamers wherever you may be
These are the finest flowers that ever my eyes did see.
Fine flowery hills and fishing dells and hunting also
At the top all of this mountain where fine flowers grow.
At the top all of the mountain where my love's castle stands
It's over-decked with ivory to the bottom of the strand.
There's arches and there's parches and a diamond stone so bright;
It's a beacon for a sailor on a dark, stormy night.
At the bottom of this mountain there runs a river clear.
A ship from the Indies did once anchor there,
With her red flags a-flying and the beating of a drum,
Sweet instruments of music and the firing of a gun.
So come all you little streamers that walks the meadows gay
And write unto my own true love wherever he may be
For his sweet lips entice me, but his tongue it tells me 'No!'
And an angel might direct us and it's where shall we go?

LITTLE BO~PEEP HAS LOST HER SHEEP

Running, Thatching, Courting, Screaming and Peeping

To follow the River Ouse would be a great perambulation through Sussex. It is complicated to define where a river begins, for a catchment area is the whole range of hills and valleys where the water flows to a river. We could start at a spring in Plummers Plain, or we could start in the wilds of Ashdown Forest. Wherever we begin, we will wander past weirs and bridges, woods and copses, meadows and villages, until we reach Barcombe. After Barcombe we will follow some right proper meanders; until the river leaves a memory of its former self in the landscape, by leaving oxbow lakes as it wanders to Hamsey. After this the river gets canalised, which straightens it somewhat, before it flows to Lewes, under that great chalk escarpment and next to the rather wonderful Cuilfail Tunnel – a tunnel which runs the A27 past the town.

From here the River Ouse flows down to Newhaven, but once upon a time it did a strange thing. Up until the sixteenth century it flowed towards Newhaven, which was then called Meeching, but then took a sharp left turn and flowed between shingle banks, parallel to the coast, till it reached the sea at the port of Seaford.

In the early sixteenth century there was much boat building along the lower reaches of the River Ouse, and the Lewes fishing fleet would sail down the river and fish the waters alongside the Seaford fleet.

From this time there comes a story, and here it is:

ELIZABETH'S RUN

In 1540 or thereabouts, a merchant of a noble family, Nicholas Pelham, lived in the town of Lewes. His wife had died, and didn't so many wives die in childbirth? It is a story that the gravestones of the time tell so eloquently.

So a new marriage was arranged, and that was with Elizabeth, a maid of about nineteen or twenty.

Elizabeth did what she had to do, without pleasure, but also without question; it's the way things were. The marriage proceeded, but she resented being spoken to as if she were a child – she was a woman, wasn't she? She had command of the household, she had to endure the sweaty attentions of the middle-aged Nicholas within the marriage chamber, she had the servants calling her mistress, and the swains touched their forelocks. She wasn't going to cower and tremble – when Nicholas ordered her around, or spoke to her as if she was an imbecile, her eyes would flash, and she would answer back sharply. Nicholas' ideas of pleasure – the picnic by the river with the servants dancing attendance, the decorous stroll through Lewes – were so tedious to her that sometimes she just wished she could run like she had as a child, to lift her skirts and fly like the wind. Not to be done of course; most unladylike.

So, when Nicholas proposed a trip down the River Ouse to Seaford, the idea was groaningly dull to her – it would mean watching the riverbanks drift slowly by, whilst her husband talked incessantly about money.

'No,' she said, 'I don't want to go.' He insisted, she protested, he insisted again. He was her husband, so it had to be. He, however, had had a gutful of her perpetual complaining, her resistance to any of his attempts at a pleasurable and civilised life; and he shouted: 'If you complain, if you will not have it, I will put you on shore.'

'Yes sir, you would have it so, sir,' she hissed into his face, hands on hips, clearly believing he never really would. Oh dear – what a provocation – something snapped in his head – the humiliation of having such an uncontrollable wife – he was suddenly filled with a hot rage, his face reddened, and he thought, 'try me, just try me.'

Off they set down the river; the sun shone, the oarsmen pulled at the sweeps, and Nicholas began to think that perhaps all would be well. Life could be gentle and decorous, she could be an obedient and worthy wife, he could bask in the respect of his peers with no thought of whispering and laughing behind his back.

'We can moor up here,' said Nicholas, as they passed a pleasant meadow, 'then we will dine in the sunshine.'

'Dine in the sunshine,' sneered Elizabeth, 'more tedium. Let us carry on to Seaford and be done with it.'

Nicholas snapped.

'I said I will put you ashore, and so I will,' he screamed; and to the consternation of the stewards and squires and ladies-in-waiting, Elizabeth was put out onto the riverbank, and the boat proceeded on down the Ouse.

'So,' thought Elizabeth, 'he thinks I will make my way back shamefaced. I will not.' She turned from the river, just as the weather broke, and a storm came howling in from the sea. Ships were driven aground from the Goodwin Sands to the cliffs of the Isle of Wight. Nicholas' pleasure boat never reached the sea; they turned her back for Lewes, whilst servants ran along the riverbank, desperately searching for Elizabeth. She was not found.

At least, she was not found by anyone from the Pelham household. She was found – soaked, freezing, and in the first stages of exposure – by a shepherd called Joshua. It was he who brought her back to his shepherd's hut and gave her sheepskins, and averted his eyes whilst she warmed herself by the fire.

It was to his surprise that she never left; that they began a strange relationship of talk and shared interest; that she took to the ways of shepherding and sheep as well as any shepherdess born to the work. It was a year before their relationship became that of a husband and wife, though they'd never so much as jumped the broomstick. She was unrecognisable as the wife of Nicholas Pelham.

And so things might have continued, were it not for the bloody French.

In 1545, a fleet led by High Admiral Claude d'Annebault was raiding down the south coast of England. At Portsmouth Henry VIII's prize ship, the *Mary Rose*, came out to engage them, and, in a terrible, freak accident, sunk as she did so. The French moved on down the coast and sacked Brighthelmstone, before heading for Meeching and Seaford.

It was Joshua, with the far-seeing eyes of a shepherd, who saw the distant smoke over Meeching; it was Joshua who then noticed the French ships working their way down the coast. He ran towards Elizabeth and the flock, for it was Elizabeth who was fleet of foot. She had to bring the warning so the local militia could be gathered. And where did she have to go? To Lewes, and the worthy Nicholas Pelham.

At first Joshua tried to prevent her – he would go – but he knew that she was as fleet as a deer, and it must be her.

And so she ran; and to this day the track up the side of the River Ouse is known as Elizabeth's Run – at least to the locals who know.

And when she stood in front of Nicholas – for several years had passed – she had lost the ivory fairness of her skin; she looked stronger, and in command of herself, so maybe he didn't recognise her. But then to recognise her he would have to admit to being a cuckold, and Nicholas abhorred being mocked. Besides, there was urgent business to attend to: the safety of England was at stake.

Nicholas gathered up an army of local townsmen, gentry and yeomen, all of whom were thoroughly sick of a lifetime of French raiding. This army, fired by rage and the desperate necessity to protect their own, fell on the French at Seaford, causing the French to retreat to their ships with considerable loss of life.

Nicholas Pelham was a hero – he had succeeded in doing what the king's flagship had failed to do; he had driven the French away. He was knighted by the king; the area of Seaford where they had defeated the French became known as 'The Buckle' after the Pelham family symbol; and after Sir Nicholas' death, a plaque was placed in St Michael's Church in Lewes bearing the inscription: 'What time the Frenche sought to have sack't Sea Foord, This Pelham did Repel'em back aboord.' So should he turn on that woman, herself a heroine, already the creator of a legend, 'Elizabeth's Run'? It would hardly be politic; and even if the law was on his side, that wouldn't prevent his status of hero changing to that of laughing stock.

She knew that he knew. He knew that she knew that he knew. She knew that he knew that she knew that he knew; but nothing was said. The Pelham family passed into history as a great local family, and for all I know their descendants might have merged years later with the descendants of Elizabeth and Joshua; but then none of us really know who all our ancestors are, because there are an awful lot of them, and genealogists only trace the ancestors they choose to.

It was after this that Seaford Harbour began to silt up, and the River Ouse was diverted straight out to the sea at Meeching, which became the New Haven. The people of Seaford took to wicked ways to earn a living, and became really rather fond of wrecking, which caused them to be known as 'Cormorants' or 'Shags'.

I find Newhaven a romantic place, and I like to watch, from beneath the low, crumbling chalk cliffs, the Dieppe-bound ferry heading full astern out of the harbour. I also like to visit the Hillcrest community centre down by the river, because they have a very good storytelling club there, called the 'Guesthouse Storytellers', and I love to listen to a good tale.

THE SPARROWS IN THE THATCH

Inland from Newhaven there is a village called Alciston. My maternal grandparents lived there, and I remember visiting as a child. Above the village there rises the dramatic rampart of Firle Beacon, and a morning walk from the secluded village up to the Downs was an exhilarating experience. I visited there recently, and talked to a couple walking their dogs, and they remembered my grandparents. 'It's all different now,' said the man. 'You don't see folk from one week to the next.' I suppose it has become a dormitory village.

This is a story from long ago, from a time of arranged marriages. Arranged marriages may now sound like a feature of Asian cultures, but they were commonplace in England in the comparatively recent past. I remember talking to an old countryman in the 1970s, who told me about his own pre-war arranged marriage, and the work of the matchmakers.

Once upon a time, in Alciston, there lived a young farm labourer. He had fallen in love with the daughter of a prosperous farmer – and she with him. They walked and they talked, and they had so much in common that they could finish each other's sentences.

But he was a labourer, and the son of a labourer, and she was the daughter of a rich farmer. The social gap was too wide for there to be any question of marriage, and when the matchmakers went to work, she was to be married to a farmer from down Selmeston way, whilst he was married to a farm worker's daughter, who was barely more than a child … and there was nothing either of them could do about it.

On the day of the wedding, all the young man thought about was the woman he loved, and when the couple got back to their cottage, he hollered and shouted at his new wife. And that was the way of the marriage – he took his bitterness out on his wife, who accepted that was the way of things; they had four children, and he took his bitterness out on them too. He even took his bitterness out on the animals he worked with. He was violent, he was hard, and he was bitter.

And so, in the village of Alciston, he was a deeply unpopular man, and surely he should have been 'rough music-ed' through the village – something we heard about in Amberley – for beating his wife. Everyone was afraid of him though, so they steered well clear.

When he was in his fifties, he woke up one day in the middle of the morning. He was a farm worker, so he was used to rising early. A 'lie-in' still meant rising at seven – to wake up mid-morning was unprecedented.

He lay there for a while, looking up at the beams under the thatched roof. Outside he could hear rain. For a while he wondered what day it was, and then remembered it was Sunday. The family were at church. Today he hadn't awoken as usual, and they must have been too afraid to wake him up. He felt a great sense of relaxation – his limbs were heavy – and the rain outside the cottage made him feel as if he was in a womb.

Then he saw a fluttering above him. He looked up and saw a sparrow frantically darting around the beams. He got up, looked more closely, and saw a nest. As he peered into it and saw two chicks, the mother flew at his face, pecking at him. He laughed; it was a morning of unexpected feelings. He was impressed with her bravery in attempting to protect her chicks. He saw then that the reason for her being so frantic was that there was a hole in the thatching, and rain was dripping onto the nest and the two bedraggled chicks.

He went out into the rain, took the ladder, and climbed onto the roof. Through the rain he could see the pointy 'hat' that sat on top of the church's stumpy tower, so typically Sussex, and he knew everyone was inside listening to the sermon, and that his place on the pew was empty. He fixed the hole in the roof, and clambered down. Going back inside, he lay down on the bed again, and gazed up at the nest. The mother sparrow had settled down.

And when the family came back from church, that was how they found his body. He was buried in the churchyard.

***

When I heard this story about Alciston, I had never come across 'Sparrows' by the great Indian writer and film maker, K.A. Abbas. Whilst swapping some stories in the courtyard of a house in Patiala, in the Indian Punjab, a boy showed me his school book for learning English. This book contained short stories, including Abbas' 'Sparrows'. In spite of the fact that, for me, the story will always be set in Alciston, I was so struck by the similarity that I suspect that Abbas' story is the source – but who knows? (There is a website link to 'Sparrows' by K.A. Abbas in the bibliography.)

THE LONG MAN OF WILMINGTON

If we wander eastwards from Alciston, we'll come to a famous Sussex landmark, the Long Man of Wilmington, that chalk figure of a giant holding two staffs, cut into the side of Windover Hill. At least they are usually interpreted as two staffs. My daughter, Ruth, when she was a little girl, saw a picture of the Long Man and immediately said, 'Oh, he's opening a door', and I thought, 'Of course, that's it, it's the king under the hill again' – or someone emerging from the other world. Stories do relate that he popped out of the hill to have a bit of a scrap with another giant, something giants are wont to do. There was at that time a giant living on the top of Firle Beacon, above Alciston, and the two giants hurled rocks at each other until the poor Wilmington giant was killed, and left the mark of his body on the side of the hill. The story of giants chucking rocks at each other seems to exist throughout the British Isles, though somehow lumps of Sussex chalk don't seem to carry the same threat as granite boulders. A flint-tipped spear would be something else entirely, though.

Another feature of the Long Man that isn't always alluded to, however, is his, well, lack of a certain length when compared to a certain Dorset giant. There is a story that explains this.

Both giants, you see, were paying court to a certain undulating beauty: the maid of the Mixon Hole. The king of the Mixon Hole, patriarch that he was, had arranged a marriage for his daughter with the Lomea Leviathan, a much-feared sea monster that lived in the dangerous and unpredictable Goodwin Sands, off the coast of neighbouring Kent. The princess of the Mixon Hole didn't fancy the match at all; she was fond of both her freedom and her home comforts, and the Lomea Leviathan was a dominating character. She really didn't want to embark on a marriage that would be a perpetual power struggle. She knew that whilst both the Cerne Abbas giant and the Long Man of Wilmington were typical of giants in being of somewhat limited intellect, they were both considered to be deities by the local yokels, and they were both capable of doing the business (she'd already ascertained that); so both were potential suitors.

The king agreed to this, but only on condition that the giants proved themselves; plainly one, in order to be a suitable husband, should prove his superiority over the other. Now the Saxon Shore has always had a connection with both the Danelaw and the Nordic north, so the king sent word that the terrible sea monster, the Kraken, should be brought down from Norway. He should pretend to hold the princess prisoner in the subterranean caverns off Beachy Head, and the giant who could rescue her would be the one to have her as his bride.

So whilst the princess and the Kraken played poker beneath Beachy Head, word was sent to the two giants that whoever rescued her would become a prince of the Mixon Hole. Both giants sallied forth from their respective down lands, but before battle could commence, there were temptations to be resisted. The temptations were sirens, a veritable shoal of beautiful, seductive mermaids, all of whom could shatter a conch shell at fifty fathoms' distance, with their wondrous soprano voices. The Dorset giant fell at the first hurdle, being led – as usual – by his appendage, but the doughty Sussex giant shut his eyes, covered his ears, and proceeded through this sea of temptation.

However, it has to be said that the Long Man wasn't the bravest giant in the land, and wouldn't anyone flee at the sight of the terrible Kraken? So when the Kraken roared, waved its tentacles and created a maelstrom, the Long Man decided that discretion was the better part of valour and beat a hasty retreat to the Sussex coast.

Now, the maid of the Mixon Hole was really quite impressed by the Kraken; though it has to be said that for someone who lived in the deep, she really was rather shallow. The king of the Mixon Hole, however, was less than impressed with both giants, and swearing that the Long Man was less than a man, he removed his manhood and gave it to the Cerne Abbas giant to add to his own. It was a cruel fate he cast on the Cerne Abbas giant, though, for that gentleman was fated to remain on the side of his Dorset hill in a perpetual state of arousal, but frozen into the turf, unable to do anything about it. Meanwhile, couples, unable to conceive, would do the business on his person, adding to his perpetual frustration. Sisyphus thought he had it bad!

The ironically named Long Man of Wilmington, however, peers timorously out of his doorway, over the Sussex Downs. He does, though, occasionally enjoy movement, and takes a bit of a wander. There are people who have seen him walk the Sussex skyline, though I'm told that these are people who have the second sight. Whatever that is.

> The story's finally finished,
> It's finally come to an end.
> I'm glad it's finally done with,
> It was driving me round the bend.

LANDSCAPE CHANGE: BEACHY HEAD TO THE PEVENSEY LEVELS

If we continue eastwards, past the wondrous and spectacular meanders of the Cuckmere river, the South Downs finally come to an end at the beautiful Seven Sisters, cliffs that look more like the White Cliffs of Dover than the White Cliffs of Dover do. Then there is Beachy Head.

> The first land we sighted was called the Dodman,
> Next Rame Head off Plymouth, off Portsmouth the Wight,
> We sailed by Beachy, by Fairlight and Dover,
> And then we bore up for the South Foreland light …

This extract comes from the sea chanty *Spanish Ladies*, for Beachy Head was a great landmark for sailors. Beachy Head isn't named after a beach; it's a corruption of the French, 'Beauchef', which means beautiful headland. It is beautiful, but it seems to have attracted a morbid, and folkloric, reputation as a suicide spot. Louis de Bernières describes this as 'a stygian form of tourism'.

It does feel dizzying at the top of the cliff, and Shakespeare's description, from *King Lear*, of gazing down from a cliff's heights, can't be surpassed:

> How fearful
> And dizzy 'tis to cast one's eyes so low!
> The crows and choughs that wing the midway air
> Show scarce so gross as beetles. Half way down
> Hangs one that gathers samphire, dreadful trade!
> Methinks he seems no bigger than his head.
> The fishermen that walk upon the beach
> Appear like mice, and yond tall anchoring bark
> Diminish'd to her cock, her cock a buoy
> Almost too small for sight. The murmuring surge,
> That on th' unnumber'd idle pebble chafes,
> Cannot be heard so high. I'll look no more,

Lest my brain turn, and the deficient sight
Topple down headlong. (*King Lear*, Act 4, Scene 6)

There are, however, those who in a practical sense have to deal with the results of such despair, and one such character, who has passed into legend, is PC Harry Ward.

PC Ward patrolled the Downs throughout the 1950s, up until 1966. He did this on his horse, Jumbo, and the two of them were a favourite sight for tourists. He was also, on all too many occasions, lowered over the cliffs of Beachy Head, using the most primitive climbing gear, in order to recover suicide victims and dogs that had fallen and got stuck on ledges. PC Ward is the perfect example of a relatively recent figure who has become a legend.

Nowadays there are people who walk Beachy Head and attempt to talk people down if they are contemplating suicide; sometimes these are people who have been in that dark place themselves. I do think that such people, along with those who 'man' (what an unfortunately gender-specific word) the Samaritans switchboards, and the switchboards of rape crisis centres or Childline, are unsung heroes.

Just beyond Beachy Head we have the resort town of Eastbourne, smaller and more sedate than Brighton; we have Eastbourne Council to thank for the preservation of Beachy Head.

In 1950, Norman Wymer wrote: 'At Eastbourne we bid farewell to the South Downs, and as we journey north-eastwards to the low-lying plain and marshes of the Pevensey Levels, we see Sussex once more in an extremely different light.' Wymer describes the barrenness and bleakness of the area and writes: 'Few will take kindly to the Pevensey Levels'; but maybe this is because it is such a contrast with a picture of Sussex as a county of chalk downs. There is a bleakness to the area though, and there is a tower in Pevensey Castle that reflects this, because the terrors, trials and tribulations of life there have stamped themselves into a face of stone.

THE PEVENSEY SCREAM

I like to walk to Pevensey Castle from Pevensey Bay. Not so long ago this walk would have been a swim, for Pevensey Castle had a commanding position on the coast before the sea retreated, stranding the castle inland. If you walk towards the castle you can watch it slowly grow bigger, and imagine yourself sailing towards the great castle by the sea.

But then, as you enter the gatehouse, there is an unsettling sight. The left-hand tower has stamped upon it a face; an expression of grief, some say a scream, fixed in crumbling stone. It is the face of the castle.

Parts of the castle are Roman – it was originally built by an upstart called Carausius, and was called Anderida. Just in case anyone gets the impression that the Roman Empire was some sort of a monolith, this story gives a different picture. Carausius defied the emperor Diocletian and had himself proclaimed emperor of Britain and a slice of Gaul. In AD 290, he constructed forts along the south-east coast in order to keep his empire safe. It didn't do him a lot of good; he was assassinated by his follower, Alectus, who forthwith proclaimed himself emperor. He got his reward when he was defeated by the armies of Diocletian.

Over the next 400 years, as Rome crumbled, Pevensey was occupied by Romano-Britons, who lost the protection of Rome. In AD 490, according to the *Anglo-Saxon Chronicle*, a Saxon raiding force besieged the fort with such ferocity that not a Briton survived the slaughter. Already there was blood, grief and anguish in the ground.

In 1066 William the Bastard, later known as the Conqueror (though you probably have to be the one in order to become the other) set up his invasion base camp here, his first foothold before he went a-harrowing across England. In 1067 he humiliated the defeated English nobility at Pevensey Castle by making a ceremonial distribution of English lands to his victorious Norman gang members.

William built the castle up, and it became a nearly invincible stronghold; no one could break their way through its defences. They could, though, starve the occupants out.

In 1088 there was another spat within the ruling class; squabbles amongst the powerful have always brought death and misery to the peasantry. After the death of William in 1087, his followers fell to fighting with each other, and the Count of Montain and Bishop Odo of Bayeux mounted a challenge to the succession. The new king, William's son Rufus the Red, who was later to die in an 'accident' in the New Forest, lay siege to the castle, with the Count and Bishop Odo holed up inside. Rufus couldn't get in, but he starved them out.

Then, in 1147, it was Gilbert de Clare, Earl of Pembroke, who was in possession of the castle, and he decided to mount a challenge against King Stephen. Once again, the king was unable to get in, but he starved the occupants out. More grief, fear and pain planted itself into the ground.

In 1204 the castle was 'slighted' by King John. He couldn't afford its upkeep, so attempted to render it unworkable as a castle. It was too solid a structure to be so easily slighted, though.

In 1264, the unslighted castle was held by forces loyal to the King Stephen, during the rebellion of Simon de Montfort. The king's forces were routed at the Battle of Lewes, and holed up in Pevensey Castle. Simon had no more luck in getting them out than any of his predecessors, and the king's loyalists held out until the wheel of fortune turned, and King Stephen was victorious.

In 1381 the peasants revolted, probably not before time, and a lot of them burned the castle's court rolls and gave the steward a very bad time. Of course the Peasants' Revolt came to a sticky end on Blackheath, but that's another story.

The final siege was in 1399. Sir John Pelham, an ancestor of Sir Nicholas Pelham, who we have already met, resided in Pevensey Castle. He supported Henry Bolingbroke in his rebellion against Richard II (there seems to be a pattern emerging). In his 1904 book *Highways and Byways of Sussex*, E.V. Lucas tells us a romantic story. Sir John was away, and Lady Joan Pelham was mistress of the castle when Richard's forces laid siege. She held out against the king's forces, but smuggled out a letter to her husband:

My dear Lord, — I recommend me to your high Lordship, with heart and body and all my poor might. And with all this I thank you as my dear Lord, dearest and best beloved of all earthly lords. I say for me, and thank you, my dear Lord, with all this that I said before of [for] your comfortable letter that you sent me from Pontefract, that came to me on Mary Magdalen's day – for by my troth I was never so glad as when I heard by your letter that ye were strong enough with the grace of God for to keep you from the malice of your enemies. And, dear Lord, if it like to your high Lordship that as soon as ye might that I might hear of your gracious speed, which God Almighty continue and increase. And, my dear Lord, if it like you to know my fare, I am here laid by in manner of a siege with the county of Sussex, Surrey, and a great parcel of Kent, so that I may not [go] out nor no victuals get me, but with much hard. Wherefore, my dear, if it like you by the advice of your wise counsel for to set remedy of the salvation of your Castle and withstand the malice of the Shires aforesaid. And also that ye be fully informed of the great malice-workers in these shires which have so despitefully wrought to you, and to your Castle, to your men and to your tenants; for this country have they wasted for a great while.

Farewell, my dear Lord! the Holy Trinity keep you from your enemies, and soon send me good tidings of you. Written at Pevensey, in the Castle, on St. Jacob's day last past.

By your own poor

J. Pelham.

Sir John leapt onto his white charger and galloped from Pontefract to Pevensey, defeated the king's forces, and rescued his wife. Oh, how these Pelhams have got themselves a good press. The letter seems so loving and romantic, it recently found its way into a book called *Love Letters of Great Women*. Historians, though, say that the J. Pelham who wrote the letter was actually Sir John himself, and the letter was written to Bolingbroke, which doesn't half change the meaning. Still, why should the facts stand in the way of a good story?

Whatever stories there may be about the heroic Pelhams, a siege brings death and misery, whether it be successful or unsuccessful. The 1399 siege was unsuccessful and Bolingbroke went on to become Henry IV; wherever did this notion about the God-given right of succession of kings and queens come from?

After this, Pevensey harbour began to silt up, and the castle slowly crumbled. As it did so, a strange thing happened. One of the gatehouse towers gave up the ghost, slumping into the Pevensey soil. The other tower twisted and froze its face into a permanent grimace of grief and horror. As you approach the bridge over the moat, with the gatehouse behind, you will see it on your left, staring blankly over the Pevensey Levels.

Leave it some flowers – show it that there is some kindness left in the world.

LITTLE BO-PEEP

Not so far from Pevensey is Ninfield; and Ninfield has always laid claim to the nursery rhyme 'Little Bo-Peep'. One story says that the sea used to come up to Ninfield, and the smugglers would come ashore there. Little Bo-Peep would take her flock up and down the beach, and erase the marks left by the smugglers. But wouldn't the sea do that? And isn't Bo Peep simply peep-bo backwards? Peep-bo – I'm watching! For the smugglers were watching for the excise men, and Bo-Peep's sheep were very likely the un-sheeplike smugglers who were bringing their tails behind them – their contraband. But Bo-Peep pops up throughout Sussex: there's a Bo-Peep Bostal (a bostal is a steep Sussex pathway) near Alciston, where folk may have watched out for the revenue officers; or maybe where the Firle giant watched out for the Long Man of Wilmington. The shepherds, too, watched over their flocks with sharp eyes, and, like Joshua, could spot a raiding French fleet from a distance; and couldn't a shepherdess peep out for her beau? Next time you go, 'peep-bo', and hide your face, think of shepherds and smugglers, the Downs and the levels, and crumbling towers that can only stare in horror. All of which brings us to the next chapter, and that eastward pointing finger of Sussex, the finger that points to the Romney Marsh.

> Little Bo-Peep has lost her sheep,
> And can't tell where to find them;
> Leave them alone, And they'll come home,
> A'bringing their tails behind them.

6

THE FAR EAST

Travelling east from the last chapter we come to the town of Battle, and the town of Hastings. The Battle of Hastings took place at Battle, not Hastings, so maybe it should be called the Hastings of Battle. King Harold Godwinson had hastened down from Stamford Bridge in Yorkshire, where he'd won a battle against the Norwegian Viking, Harald Hardrada. Harald had actually been fighting in alliance with Harold Godwinson's brother, Tostig Godwinson, which demonstrates what a lot of mafia-like family feuding all this nonsense was really comprised of.

On arrival in Sussex, Harold and his army were knackered, so they got clobbered by William the Bastard and his Normans. We've already seen, at Pevensey, that William was fond of building castles, and it was natural that he would want to build one in the Hastings area, to celebrate his victory. So a stone castle was completed in 1070. I have a feeling that, at this point, we may be leaving history and entering folklore; though history is so much based on interpretation that it could be a mistake to view them as being entirely separate.

WILLIAM'S TOES

At this time William was in the habit of staying in bed all morning; after all, he was a conqueror and could do what he wanted. One morning at eleven o'clock, though people didn't measure time with such precision in those days, William was lying in bed, listening to people outside working, and smelling the smell of the bacon, because his wife, Matilda, was making bacon sarnies for breakfast.

'I like being a conquering king,' thought William, 'because I can stay in bed for as long as I want, and if anyone tells me to get up, I'll have their heads chopped off.'

Now William had very big feet, so big they stuck out of the end of his blankets, and as he lay there, looking at his feet, he had a strange feeling. He felt that his feet were looking back at him. No, not possible. Just then, though, the big toe on the right foot said, 'What are you looking at?'

The conqueror gazed at his toe in dumb astonishment.

'I said: what are you looking at? I don't like you looking at me – you're ugly,' said the toe.

'NO ONE SPEAKS TO ME LIKE THAT – I'M KING, I'M A CONQUEROR.'

'You're just a big bully,' said the toe, 'I don't like it on your feet – they stink. I want to go home.'

'That's right,' said the big toe on the other foot, 'chop us off, and we'll go home.'

'What do you mean, chop you off?' expostulated William (he was fond of expostulating). 'You're part of my body.'

The toe explained that they used to belong to King Alfred, who was an altogether civilised Saxon, rather than a nasty Norman, and who used to wash his feet three times a day, whereas William never washed them at all. Quite naturally the toes wanted to get back to Alfred.

'I'M NOT CHOPPING OFF MY OWN TOES,' roared William, who was as fond of roaring as he was of expostulating.

'Listen, I want to ask you a question,' said the big toe on the right foot.

If you, dear reader, have been patient enough to last this long, I would like to ask you the same question. Have you ever had a drink or two before going to bed? Then in the middle of the night you wake up, and oh dear me, you're bursting for a pee. The trouble is, you're snug and comfortable, more asleep than awake, and it seems like such an effort to get out of bed. You try to go back to sleep – but everything you think about, everything you dream about (dripping taps and the like) keeps coming back to the fact that you're busting for a pee. In the end you get up, and, en route to the toilet, you stub your toe on something; I think the worst thing is the edge of a door. Well the toe asked William the Conqueror the same thing, though it didn't mention dripping taps, because they hadn't been invented.

'Happens to me all the time,' said William, 'I go quaffing mead in the mead hall with all the nobles, then in the middle of the night I've got to get up and go to the garderobe.'

Now, a garderobe is a toilet that sticks out over the edge of the castle wall. You sit on it, do the business, and it all goes flying down the outside of the castle. If you're a soldier, on sentry duty, you've got to be careful where you stand; because you never know what nasty stuff might descend on you. (This, by the way, is the reason why Normans wore pointy helmets.)

'On the way to the garderobe,' continued William, 'I stub my toe – its agony, a damn sight worse than getting an arrow in the eye.'

'Well, chop us off,' said the toe, 'and it'll never happen again.'

'That's true,' mused William, 'but no, that's silly, I wouldn't chop off my own toes.'

'Do you like dancing?' enquired the other big toe.

'Oh, I love to dance. I go down to the great hall, and dance the night away with my wife, the fair and beautiful Queen Matilda.'

Now, Queen Matilda was considered to be one of the most beautiful women in Normandy and all its territories; and in those days, quite properly, beauty was measured in pounds and ounces, so the most beautiful woman also had to be the largest and the most fullumptious. Queen Matilda had been the reason behind the widening of many a Norman arch.

'Sometimes, when we're dancing, she steps on my toe, and, especially when she's wearing her wellies, it is agony.'

'Well, chop us off,' said the toe, 'and it'll never happen again.'

'That's true,' said the mighty conqueror, 'but it's still foolish. You're my toes; I'm not chopping you off.'

Then the toe on the right foot said something you should never say to a conqueror: 'You're frightened, you're scared.'

'Cowardy, cowardy, custard, stick your head in the mustard.'

'I'M WILLIAM THE CONQUEROR, AND I'M AFRAID OF NOTHING,' bellowed the enraged conqueror, and, picking up his sword, which he kept in the bed next to his teddy bear, he swung it in a great shining arc and chopped off his two big toes. It was horrible; there was blood everywhere, and he had to tear off bits of the sheets and tie them round the stumps where the toes used to be. The strangest thing, though, happened to the toes. Little faces appeared on the toenails, and they grew tiny little arms, tiny little legs, with knees and feet, and toes of their own. They started to run round and round the room, shouting, 'We're going back to Alfred, we're going back to Alfred,' before tearing down the spiral staircase, through the kitchen, and off down the long road to Winchester (obviously the South Downs Way).

Matilda wondered what had just hurtled through the kitchen, but she finished frying the bacon, and shouted up the stairs, 'William, breakfast's ready, get out of bed, you lazy king.'

'Coming dear, coming,' replied William, who was regretting having chopped off his toes, because his feet were hurting.

Now, the thing with toes is that they don't seem to have much purpose, but if you stand up and lean forward, you will find that there is a reflex action, whereby your big toes grip the ground and help you keep your balance (I don't know what the other toes are for, probably a relic of the time when our ancestors swung through the primeval glades of the Ashdown and St Leonard's forests). So when the mighty conqueror stood up and leaned forward, he fell flat on his face with a crash.

'What on earth is going on?' muttered Matilda, and stamped up the stairs, only to find her conquering husband lying flat on his face on the floor.

'I wish I'd never chopped off my toes,' wailed William the Conqueror. 'My feet are hurting.'

'You stupid king,' shouted Matilda, 'now I'll have to go and get them,' and off she thundered, down the spiral staircase, through the kitchen, and down the road after the toes. Now, I don't think she would ever have caught them – because she did get out of breath rather quickly – but the toes got to a crossroads somewhere round about Peppering Eye Farm, and they started to argue about which was the right road to Winchester. One said they should go to the left via Twisly and Ninfield, and the other said they should go to the right, via Steven's Crouch and Brownbread Street. Well, they fell to fighting; their little fisties were flying, and they even started to kick each other. Just then, Matilda came thundering down the road and shouted triumphantly: 'GOTCHA!'

Back she went to the Norman keep, up the stairs, into the bedroom, and stuck the toes back onto the mighty conqueror's feet. The tiny little arms disappeared, the tiny little legs disappeared, and the tiny little faces disappeared. 'Quick,' she said, 'get your Norman shoes and socks on,' and so he did – and never again did he ever take them off; not when he went to bed, not even when he had a bath. And if you don't believe me, I can prove it's true. Go to your local library and look for books about the Norman Conquest. Look through all the pictures, even look through the Bayeux Tapestry if you want, and you'll never see a picture of William the Conqueror without his shoes and socks on.

And that proves that my story is true.

Not that it did the rest of England much good – he still imposed forest law, he still harried the north, and his feet still stank.

Worms and maggots
Bluebottle pies
I tells my story,
And I tells no lies.

… And now a confession.

This is an adaptation (and elongation) of a story written by the great Irish storyteller, John Campbell. What it illustrates is something very telling about stories that enter the oral vernacular. It is easy enough to transpose a story and change the locations, and traditional stories constantly change their geography, but something else happened here.

John Campbell's story was about the great Irish writer Patrick Kavanagh. In the story, there is an inspired teacher who sends a girl out looking for information about Brian Boru; the toes belong to him. She goes to Patrick Kavanagh for the information, and he sits down, has a smoke, and tells a story. I heard the story from the storyteller Doreen McBride, who comes from Banbridge town in the County Down. One day, in Sussex, I was caught a story short. 'We would like a story about William the Conqueror, because we are "doing" the Normans,' a teacher announced to me as I entered a school for a day's storytelling. I adapted the story that was rattling around in my head. I then told it so many times that I quite forgot where it came from. Then, recently, I came across a book: *A Sense of Love, A Sense of Place*, edited by Doreen McBride, and there was the story by John Campbell, and I was reminded, slightly guiltily, of hearing the story from Doreen all those years ago. Sometimes a story adapts, morphs, shifts through a combination of circumstances, serendipity, the sudden need for a tale, the evolution through retellings, the feedback from listeners – and this shapes, reforms, and mutates the tale. This is what happened here. So if you, dear reader, take a story from this book and tell it, and you find it changing – not through a conscious process of alteration, but just because it does – let it happen, the story needs the exercise.

The Giant of Brede

North of Hastings, east of Battle, in between Cackle Street and Groaning Bridge, we come to the village of Brede. Once upon a time, in Brede, there lived a giant. This giant was not an amiable dunderhead, like Bevis of Arundel or the Long Man of Wilmington; this giant was seriously nasty.

Now, I think that in previous chapters I may have given a rather unfair impression of the maid of the Mixon Hole – portraying her as being rather undiscriminating in her choice of men. It is true that she had a bit of a thing for giants, but not just any giant would do; she certainly wanted nothing to do with the giant of Brede, for he was a disgusting creature. He'd pick his nose, and throw boulder-sized bogies around the place; he'd scratch his arse and sniff his fingers; he'd burp, fart, hawk and flob – and he'd eat children. He'd pick them up, bite off their heads, drink their blood, crunch the bones, and then pick the bits out from between his teeth.

Nowadays society teaches everyone to think of their own individual wants and desires, and then expects schools to teach cooperation – but of course cooperation is only really taught by that strict teacher, necessity. It was necessity that persuaded the children of Sussex to band together to deal with the hideous giant of Brede. So little Jim Pulk – later to gain fame by slaying a knucker – came all the way up from Lyminster, and baked a Sussex Pond Pudding. Now I know I said, when describing Jim's making of a Churdle Pie in Chapter Two, that this isn't a recipe book; but Pond Pudding is so exquisitely Sussex – the Sussex that existed before the incomers brought bistros with fettuccine and olives, and tomatoes that they insist on telling us are 'vine ripened', that I have to include the complete recipe of this thoroughly healthy food. This is from the Revd Parish's *Dictionary of Sussex Dialect*; but it has been necessary for me to increase the amount of ingredients, to reflect the size of the pudding that Jim made.

> Rub 2 hundredweight of lard into ½ ton of flour.
> Add a shovelful of salt, 2 barrels of sugar, and a couple of buckets of currants.
> Mix and make into a stiff paste with milk and water.
> Take about a quarter of it and roll into a square.
> Put a gurt massive gob of butter in the middle, and roll into a ball.

Put into a greased trough and boil for 1½ days.

Turn into a dew pond, cut a round hole in the middle and stir in thirty seven bottles of blackberry wine, fifteen gallons of Sussex nettle beer, and a few sacks of brown sugar.

Replace the bit cut out and it is ready to serve.

The children placed the pie outside the giant's residence, Brede Place, and after he'd pulled a particularly large bogy out of his nose, the aroma of the pudding came wafting up his newly vacated nostril.

'What's this?' he roared, looking at the pudding, and, having no more sense than the Lyminster Knucker, he began to spoon it into his mouth. 'Yum, scrumptious, bumptious, yumptious,' spluttered the giant, cramming more and more pudding into his enormous gob. Then he looked round for something to wash it down with, and there was a trough full of huckle-my-puff, a most delicious beverage composed of eggs, beer and brandy. He downed that, and polished off the pud. The ale, wine and brandy did its work, and the giant became drowsy. 'I be quotted,' he gurgled, and he lay down on his back and commenced snoring.

The children set to work, tying him up and pegging him down. They then took a great cross-cut saw of the type used by many a Sussex woodsman's team, and with the children from West Sussex on the left, and the children from East Sussex on the right, for weren't his feet pointing towards the sea, they commenced sawing.

'Oh,' gurgled the giant, 'that's my kiddlies.'

The children sawed faster.

'Oh,' spluttered the giant, 'that's my liver.'

The children sawed faster.

'Oh,' groaned the giant, 'that's my sausages.'

The children sawed faster.

'Oh,' moaned the giant, 'this is offal; my lights are going out,' and he promptly expired.

The children cheered, the giant was sawn in half – and that was the end of him.

And as far as I'm concerned, it served him right.

Yum yum,
Pig's bum,
Yo ho,
The story's done.

DOWN TO THE MARSHES FROM RYE

Travelling further east we come to two hilltop towns: Winchelsea and Rye.

These are towns that belong in another world, and whose history lies about them more due to the towns themselves than the efforts of the heritage industry. Esther Meynell, in her book *Sussex*, quotes Shakespeare's Prospero when she describes the windows of Rye gazing into 'the dark backward and abysm of Time'; and the image is particularly appropriate because of the towns' island-like qualities. Like Pevensey, both these towns, with their harbours, once stood on the seashore, but the sea has since retreated, leaving flat, marshy land behind. Meynell writes that when mists come up from the sea, 'Rye seems to float in the air like a town in a mirage'; something that Turner captured in his painting *Rye, Sussex*.

But if Rye gazes southwards over relatively recent marshland to the sea, it gazes eastwards over the much more ancient Romney Marsh.

The Romney Marsh is mostly in Kent, but there is a substantial slice in Sussex. Maybe, though, Romney Marsh is neither in Kent or Sussex; maybe it's not even in England. Thomas Ingoldsby, in *The Ingoldsby Legends*, writes: 'There's Europe, Ashy, Africa, America – and Romney Marsh.' And there are creatures in the marsh.

There is the Wish Hound – and isn't 'wish' a Sussex dialect word for marsh? This terrible black dog will follow you in the lonely lanes at night, and it will bring ill fortune. But then, could not this beast be the spirit of disease and sickness? In the late Middle Ages the marsh was devastated by the Black Death, and even if much of the rest of England suffered the same fate, malaria and other water-borne diseases wrought more misery on the marsh people; mortality rates on the marsh were twice as high as in villages just a few miles away. So the marsh was an unhealthy place, and the web-footed inhabitants had to survive by their own independent and lawless skills. They were smugglers before smuggling was invented. The classic period of smuggling involved importing goods into the country, and paying no duty on it, but in Romney Marsh the owlers had exported fine Sussex wool to the weavers of Flanders since the thirteenth century, so they took readily to any form of smuggling that presented itself. Dealing with Flanders, France or England; it was all the same to them. The marsh people owed no allegiance to politicians or monarchs; they owed allegiance to each other, and to survival. So Romney Marsh was always a contradiction: a remote, obscure, hidden place, but at the same time an important place; a frontier between countries.

So Wish Hounds, owlers, signals in the darkness, corpse candles, Jackie lanterns, mawkin heads – all could be out on the Romney Marsh at night. And then there's Elynge Ellet; she was always the worst.

In the Sussex dialect the ellet is the elder bush, and elynge means a solitary, uncanny, eerie place – and Elynge Ellet was a creature that lived in the marsh; a green-toothed, green-haired, frog-eyed creature with long fingers like suckers, and woe betide the children who played beside a marsh pond, because Elynge Ellet might get them.

ELYNGE ELLET

Once upon a time there was an owler, and he had done well out of the wool trade and had become prosperous; but then he fell on hard times. Quite why he did so I don't know, but what I do know is that the poorer he got, the poorer he got. Maybe there would be a hole in the roof, and he couldn't afford to fix it, and the rain would get in and damage the little wool he had, and so things went from bad to worse, and from worse to even worse than that.

One day he was walking around a marsh pond, muttering, 'I wish I was rich again; I wish I was rich again.' At first the water was still, but then it started to bubble and boil, and bubble and boil, and out came Elynge Ellet, with her long green hair, green slithery-slithery teeth, frogs' eyes, and long fingers like suckers.

'So,' she said, in a voice like the croaking of frogs, 'You'd like to be rich again?'

'Um, yes,' he answered, naturally somewhat stunned.

'Well, it can be so,' said she, 'but every spell has another side to it.' (I believe this is known as 'There's no such thing as a free lunch'.) 'You would have to give me the youngest living thing in your cottage.'

'The cat's just had kittens,' thought the owler, 'that's a good bargain'; so he agreed.

'Don't forget, don't forget,' croaked Elynge Ellet, and ebbed back into the pond.

As the owler approached his cottage, the old midwife came hobbling out, screeching, 'Good news, good news; your wife has just given birth to a lovely bouncing baby boy.'

'That can't be!' cried the owler. 'The baby wasn't due for another two or three weeks' – but it was; so we know what the youngest living thing in the owler's cottage was – the owler's own son. He told the midwife what had happened.

'What shall I do?'

'Just keep the baby away from the marsh pond.'

Well, it's easy enough to keep a baby away from a pond – but the baby grew older, and the baby became a toddler. The spell seemed to be working, because the owler was growing richer. He wasn't growing happier, however, because he was worried that Elynge Ellet would come and get the toddler. They always kept the toddler away from the marsh pond, and the toddler grew older and became a little boy.

They always told him, 'KEEP AWAY FROM THE MARSH POND.'

The owler grew richer, but not happier.

The little boy grew older, and became a big boy; and they always told him, 'KEEP AWAY FROM THE MARSH POND.'

The owler grew richer, but not happier.

The big boy grew older until he became a young man, and he was a handsome and hardworking young man, and also a great hunter.

One day the king came riding by, and whether he was the king of Sussex, the king of Kent, the king of England, or the king of the marsh, I can't say, but he rode at the head of a splendid procession of courtiers, all dressed in their finery, and the king announced, 'Owler, I would like your son to come and work for me at the court, and be my chief hunter.'

'Wonderful,' thought the owler, 'my son working for the king, wouldn't that make me important – and I won't need to worry about Ellynge Ellet any more.'

So the young man went to work for the king, and that was fine. And the young man met a young woman, and that was fine; and they fell in love, and that was fine; and they were married, and that was fine.

One day the young man was galloping along on his horse in pursuit of a hare. He took his bow, pulled back the bow string, shot the arrow, and killed the hare. He dismounted and took out his knife, thinking that if he skinned the hare he could take the meat home for the pot, and out of the fur he could make a lovely pair of slippers for his wife.

So he skinned and gutted the hare, and there was blood on his hands, and he thought, 'Now, where is the nearest place to wash my hands?' and of course – it would be, wouldn't it? – it was the marsh pond.

He washed his hands, and at first all was quiet except for the croak of a frog and the pop of a bubble to the surface. But then the water started to …

> Bubble and boil
> And
> bubble and boil

… and out came Elynge Ellet with her long green hair, green slithery-slithery teeth, frogs' eyes, and long fingers like suckers. She flung her arms around the young man and dragged him into the pond, then all the water fell back, and all was quiet again. Now, another young man had been hunting with him and saw this. He galloped back to the young man's wife, shouting, 'Terrible, terrible news – Elynge Ellet's got your husband.'

The young woman ran to the mill pond, and she ran round and round, saying: 'Elynge, Elynge Ellet, give me back my husband,' but there was nothing. After a long while, she was exhausted, and she lay down by the pond and fell fast asleep.

When she was asleep she had a dream.

She dreamed that she was treading through a swamp on the very far side of Sussex, and in the swamp there was a rickety-rackety wooden hut. She knocked on the door, and Old Nan answered.

'Yes, my dear?' said the old woman.

'I'm looking for my husband; Elynge Ellet has got him.'

'Ah, Elynge, Elynge Ellet. There's only one thing you can do now, my dear. Take a silver comb and go down to the pond on a night of the big full moon, and comb your hair with the silver comb, comb your hair with the silver comb, comb your hair …' and the young woman woke up. 'It was just a dream, all a dream, and I thought I had someone on my side, someone to help me.' But then she looked beside her, and there was a silver comb.

So, on a night when the big full moon was in the sky, down she went to the marsh pond, and she combed her hair with the silver comb, and at first there wasn't a sound except for the croak of a frog, and the pop of a bubble to the surface, but then the water started to …

Bubble and boil
And
bubble and boil

… and out came Elynge Ellet with her long green hair, green slithery-slithery teeth, frogs' eyes, and long fingers like suckers.

The young woman could see her husband's head sticking out of the water – just his head – and she could hear him calling, 'Help me, help me,' but Elynge said 'Noooo…', and pushed his head under the water, and a great wave grew from the ripples and took the silver comb, and washed it into the pond. Then all the water fell back, and there wasn't a sound, except for the pop of a bubble to the surface, and the croak of a frog.

'Elynge, Elynge Ellet, Give me back my husband,' called the young woman, but there was nothing.

For a while, what she did, or where she went, I don't know. But one night she was exhausted, and she lay down by the pond, and she fell fast asleep.

She dreamed that she was treading through the swamp, and in the swamp there was the rickety-rackety wooden hut. She knocked on the door, and Old Nan answered.

'Hello, my dear, have you come to give me back my silver comb?'

'No.'

'No?'

'Elynge's got it. Elynge Ellet's got it.'

'Ah, Elynge, Elynge Ellet. There's only one thing you can do now, my dear. Take a magic reed pipe, and go down to the pond on a night of the big full moon, and play a tune on the pipe, play a tune on the pipe, play …' and the young woman woke up.

'Was it a dream?' she thought, but there next to her was a little reed pipe, so, on a night when the big full moon was in the sky, down she went to the marsh pond, and she played the pipe, and at first there wasn't a sound except for the sound of the pipe, and the croak of a frog, and the pop of a bubble to the surface, but then the water started to …

Bubble and boil
And
bubble and boil

… and out came Elynge Ellet with her long green hair, green slithery-slithery teeth, frogs' eyes, and long fingers like suckers, and there was the young woman's husband; she could see him from the waist up, and he was calling out, 'help me, help me please!', but Elynge said 'Noooo…', and pushed his head under the water, and a great wave grew from the ripples, and took the magic pipe, and washed it into the pond. Then all the water fell back, and there wasn't a sound, except for the pop of a bubble to the surface, and the croak of a frog.

'Elynge, Elynge Ellet, Give me back my husband,' called the young woman, but there was nothing.

For a while, what she did, or where she went, I don't know. But one night she was exhausted, and she lay down by the pond, and she fell fast asleep.

She dreamed that she was treading through the swamp, and in the swamp there was the rickety-rackety wooden hut. She knocked on the door, and Old Nan answered.

'Hello, my dear, have you come to give me back my magic pipe?'

'No.'

'No?'

'Elynge's got it. Elynge Ellet's got it.'

'Ah, Elynge, Elynge Ellet. There's only one thing you can do now, my dear. Take a spinning wheel, and go down to the pond on a night of the big full moon, and spin and spin with the spinning wheel, and when you've finished spinning: Dance …

> And dance around that spinning wheel
> Dance around that spinning wheel
> Dance around …

… and the young woman woke up, and there, of course, was a spinning wheel. So she took the spinning wheel and, on a night when the big full moon was in the sky, down she went to the marsh pond and she spun and spun on the spinning wheel, and when she'd finished spinning, she danced …

> And she danced around that spinning wheel
> Danced around that spinning wheel

… and at first there wasn't a sound except for the flip-flap, flip-flap of her bare feet on the wet grass, and the croak of a frog, and the pop of a bubble to the surface, but then the water started to …

> Bubble and boil
> And
> bubble and boil

... and out came Elynge Ellet with her long green hair, green slithery-slithery teeth, frogs' eyes, and long fingers like suckers, and there was the young woman's husband, all of him, and he was hurled out of the pond, and she flung her arms around him, and he flung his arms around her, and she said, 'It's alright, I've got you, I've got you,' but Elynge shouted, 'NO!', and dropped a wave on the two of them, and washed them into a pond. In the pond, Elynge Ellet cast a spell and turned her into a toad and him into a frog, and spat them out into separate parts of the high downs. Up on the Downs they both became themselves again, but Elynge had cast a worse spell – for she had taken away their memories, and they couldn't remember who they were, or what they were, or why they were.

Up on the Downs they both became shepherds, and on their travels in those wide, airy, open spaces of chalk and flint, they met each other, but they didn't know each other because their memories were gone. They became great friends and put their sheep together into one flock, and one day he sat by the flock playing a pipe, and she started to remember a time when she'd played a pipe by a pond, and slowly the memories started to return to her – then faster and faster, as if the flood gates had been opened. She began to cry, and he said, 'What's the matter, why are you crying?' and she said, 'Don't you know?' and he said, 'No,' and then one of the tears fell on him, and the memories started to flood back into his head – and he remembered who he was, and they fell into each other's arms.

And so they went back to the marsh, and maybe – maybe – they lived happily ever after.

But I'll bet he never went near that marsh pond again.

Just in case.

Into the West

Now, should you ever read *Grimm's Fairy Tales*, you might come across the story of the Nixie in the Millpond. It seems to be remarkably similar. But the Nixie is a beautiful water nymph, probably because the Brothers Grimm, unconsciously, wanted to give her a bit of an erotic frisson (assuming they have a problem with green teeth and the rest). But what is a Nixie? Well the Nixie is a shapeshifting water dweller, and in Old English she was known as the nicor, and what did that become in Sussex? The knucker. So this demonstrates that all stories come from Sussex; or maybe everything stems from the Romney Marsh.

And it would be good to travel further eastwards into the marsh, to all those places past Camber; to Lydd and Walland Marsh, to Coldharbour Farm and Dymchurch, and maybe way out to Dungeness nuclear power station and Derek Jarman's garden. But that takes us into Kent, even though the marsh may consider itself to be neither Kent nor Sussex, so we'd better start turning north-westwards, in order to continue on our rather elongated widdershins circumambulation of Sussex. We are heading into the Weald.

TALES OF BONES AND THE CLODGY SLAB

The High Weald

The Weald covers most of Sussex north of the Downs, and its beauty has been less eulogised than that of the South Downs; but it is lovely (well, most of it).

The word 'weald' means wilderness, or forest, and at one time it was a vast tract of forest, covering rolling hills; and it was this forest that caused Saxon Sussex to be so remote. By the end of the fourteenth century it was an area of scattered farmsteads, patches of woodland of a variety of sizes, irregularly shaped fields, open heaths, ancient route ways … and …

MUD

Sussex mud was famous. The apocryphal story is of an eighteenth-century traveller who saw a hat in a Sussex lane. He picked it up, and was surprised to find a man underneath. On digging out the man, it was found he was sitting on a horse. The traveller and his companions wondered whether the horse would survive, but the newly excavated farming gentleman said that the horse was well fed, for wasn't he eating hay from the haywain that was beneath him.

Mud was such a feature of Sussex life that, as the Inuit are reputed to have many different names for varying types of snow, so Sussexonians had many different words for different types of mud:

1. CLEDGY: earth sticking to the spade when digging wet mud.
2. CLODGY: muddy and wet, like a field path after heavy rain.
3. GAWM (GORM, GARM): especially sticky, foul-smelling mud.
4. GORMED UP: stuck, seized with mud.
5. GRABBY: grimy, filthy with mud.
6. GROM: to make dirty or muddy.
7. GUBBER: black anaerobic mud of rotting organic matter.
8. HIKE (IKE): a mess or an area of mud.
9. PAUNCH: to break up fairly coherent mud, as in 'those cows, they do paunch about the mud so'.
10. POACH: to tread the muddy ground into holes, as cattle do.
11. PUG: a kind of loam – particularly the sticky yellow Wealden clay.

12.   SLAB: the thickest mud.

13.   SLABBY: sticky, slippery, greasy, dirty mud.

14.   SLEECH: mud or river sediment used for manure – especially from the River Rother.

15.   SLOB: thick mud.

16.   SLOBBY: a state of muddiness where it is difficult to extricate the boot at each step, 'the way here was very wearisome through dirt and slobbiness'.

17.   SLOMMOCKY: made dirty with mud.

18.   SLOUGH (SLOGH): a muddy hole.

19.   SLUB: thick mud – used as slush is elsewhere.

20.   SLUBBER: to slip in mud.

21.   SLUBBY: dirty with stiff and extremely tenacious mud.

22.   SLUB-UP: to make stiff with mud, as in 'he come home all of a slub'.

23.   SLURRY: diluted mud distinct from slub; saturated with so much water that it cannot drain, churned up into a cream or paste with water.

24.   SMEERY: wet and sticky surface mud; not clodgy or slobby.

25.   SPANNEL: to make dirty with mud, as would a spaniel on a floor.

26.   STABBLE: to walk thick mud into the house.

27.   STOACH: to trample ground, like cattle; also refers to the silty mud at Rye Harbour.

28.   STOACHED: an entry to a field in bad weather is often stoached (and poached).

29.   STOACHY: dirty, mildly muddy.

30.   STODGE: thick puddingy mud.

31.   STUG: watery mud.

32.   STUGGY: filled with watery mud.

33.   SWANK: a bog.

That's thirty-three of them, but many of the folk who could tell you more are now laid beneath the stodgy slob, and we'll have to rely on the collections of the Revd Parish, and his wonderful *Dictionary of Sussex Dialect*.

Before I embark on the first story, it has been necessary for me to talk about Sussex mud; it is now also necessary for me to talk about the Hawkhurst Gang.

THE HAWKHURST GANG

In the north-east of Sussex the High Weald crosses into Kent, and it was from Hawkhurst in the Kentish weald that there came a gang of smugglers who serve to contradict the widely held belief that smugglers were romantic. The Hawkhurst Gang terrorised Sussex, and they'd spend a lot of their time in the Mermaid Inn in Rye, where they would drink with their weapons laid on the table, taking occasional pot shots at randomly chosen targets.

They extended their reign of terror so far that they crossed the length of Sussex, the width of Hampshire, and raided the custom house in Poole, Dorset. After a number of murders, however, they were finally brought down in a pitched battle in Goudhurst, Kent. Four of them met the drop at Tyburn, two in Kent, and the rest somewhere just north of Chichester (the bodies of two of them were gibbeted in what is now called Gibbet Field, in Selsey Bill).

To relate all the activities of the Hawkhurst Gang isn't actually that interesting – something to do with the banality of evil: it just seems sordid. However, they had a very malign effect on the following story, so I thought I'd better introduce them.

THE DANCING PRINCESS

Once upon a time in the county of Hampshire, the travelling people were camped around the lanes of Wickham; all there for the horse fair. Among them was a young man, and he was dashing and handsome and a great horseman – really a bit flash, and not a little arrogant. He'd bought a string of horses at Wickham Fair, and he knew he would get a good profit for them at Horsmonden Fair in Kent. He had a light trap – a fast cart – pulled by a beautiful skewbald horse; and if I'm to think of a modern equivalent I can only compare it to a sports car – this young man was flash.

> The coloured horses, the pride and joy
> Of each and every Romani boy.
> To have a race, the greatest thrill,
> On road and heath with prowess and skill.
> At a spanking pace, they come up the lane,
> With tousled hair and a flying mane.

With his grey and trap, and a string of horses, he travelled the whole width of Sussex (and Sussex is a county whose distance lies in its width), and sold the horses for a good profit. So there he was on the long journey back.

Well, the tarmacked roads, the suburbanisation of Sussex, has shrunk the county no end. But as we know, Sussex was once noted more for its pug, its terrible slobby slab; its mud. So it was a long journey being taken by our young Romani prince; and rather than tarry in Horsmonden, he started late, meaning to travel through the night. He had a pocket full of gold coins, and he was happy with the success of his mission.

Travelling through Wealden forest, lulled by the sound of hoof beats and the jingle of the harness, he thought he could hear music – the sound of a fiddle. This was strange, deep in the forest, and he pulled up his horse and listened. It was fiddle music; and Sussex folk weren't particularly given to the fiddle, and certainly not to music this fluid. This was Romani music.

The young man couldn't imagine what people were camped out here in the Weald, and it seemed only polite to find out. So he tethered his horse to a tree, and made his way into the forest. He walked quietly – for some clans were rivals and he couldn't be certain of a welcome. As the fiddle music grew louder, he saw a flicker of firelight through the trees, and then before him was the whole scene. Sitting on a tree stump, playing a fiddle, was a man with long, black, curling hair – and a look of almost demoniacal concentration. Dancing round the fire were Romani folk, but it was one young woman who mesmerised the Romani prince. She had a red dress, and with her long, black hair swirling, she whirled and danced around the fire.

'She's the one,' he thought, 'she's the one to be mine – she's the one to be my princess.'

It didn't occur to him that she might have a say in the matter – he was a prince, and he'd made a vow.

Now, surely he should have stepped out into the firelight and introduced himself – but, and he hardly knew why, he stayed hidden amongst the trees, and waited till the first grey light of morning touched the tree tops.

Then the fiddler and the dancers finally stopped, and they all crawled into a large bender tent: a tent made from withies – flexible branches of hazel – and covered with sailcloth.

'Now,' thought the young man, 'She'll come away with me.'

He crept towards the tent, but as he crawled into the darkness a terrible smell assailed his nostrils; the smell of death. As his eyes adjusted to the darkness he saw, all around him, bits and pieces of bodies – heads, arms, legs and torsos. Now you or I would have turned tail and fled, but the young man was a prince, and he'd made a vow. Although his head reeled with the horror of it all, he found the bits of body that were hers – he knew by the fragments of red dress – and stuffed them into a sack.

'If she can't be mine by day,' he thought, 'she can still be mine by night.'

He fled back to the horse and trap, whipped up the horse, and headed for Hampshire. Somehow he knew that he had to reach home by nightfall, or all would be ill.

But most of the width of Sussex in a day? Who could do that? And there were those slubby Sussex lanes; and then it started to rain. There was a farmer's cart that had lost a wheel, and he had to help get the wheel on in order to get the cart out of the way; and finally he was in Hampshire, and approaching the place where his people were encamped. But they weren't in sight before the sun went down in the west, and the moon was in the sky, and there she was, next to him.

'What are you doing?' she cried. 'What are you doing?'

'You are the one,' he shouted. 'You shall be my bride, my princess.'

'I cannot; I am of the dead. You cannot have one who is of the dead. Anyway, my brothers will come for me.'

And there they were, the three of them, riding straight and true, untrammelled by mud and rain, as only spectral horsemen can be. They circled the horse and trap, and threw the young man from it; then they beat him senseless.

When he came to, the horse and trap were still there, and his pockets were still full of money, so he hadn't been attacked by robbers. He dragged himself onto the trap, and the horse took him back to his people – back to mum.

He had to be nursed back to health, and his mother told him, sternly and angrily, that he could not have one who was of the dead.

But he had made a vow, and he was a young man obsessed. It wasn't long before he'd picked the lightest yet strongest trap, the horse that most effectively balanced speed and stamina, and set off again for the High Weald of East Sussex.

He knew the place; his eyes were alert to the shape of trees, the bend in a path, the gradient of a slope. He reined in the horse, and there, sure enough, was the sound of the fiddle. He tied the horse to a tree with a slip knot and followed the music into the darkness. The flicker of fire, the music becoming louder – and there they were. The fiddle player sat on the stump, sawing away at his violin; and there she was, wildly dancing around the fire. He waited till the morning light, watched them crowd into the tent, and then, himself, crept into that terrible place.

And there, all on that terrible ground,
Legs, bodies and limbs lay all scattered around.

He found the bits that were hers, put them into a sack – and went back, fast as he could, to the horse and trap, and away. This time he swore he would make it by nightfall – but once again it started to rain, and once again that Sussex mud sucked at the horse's hooves and the wheels of the trap; and the River Ouse was in spate, and at nightfall the young man saw the lights of his people in the lanes near Wickham, but he wasn't yet there, and night had fallen, and there she was sitting next to him – and she was staring at him in horror.

'You cannot – I am of the dead.'

'You will be mine – you will be my princess.'

'My brothers will come.'

And there they were, circling the horse and trap, and they flung him from the trap and they beat him and beat him till he was senseless.

Once again it was back to mum. 'Now it has happened twice you must have learned your lesson; you cannot have one who is of the dead.' But who learns their lesson? This is why stories with neat morals at the end are such a self-delusion – and anyway, things in stories have to happen three times.

This time the young man didn't take a horse and trap, just a horse: the fastest, lightest, strongest horse; a Scudder. Back to the forest he went, tethered the horse to a tree and disappeared into the trees. There was the fire, there the fiddler, there the dancers – and there she was – the wildest dancer of them all, spinning and whirling in her red dress.

At the first light of morning, they all went into the bender tent – and in he went, scooping up the bits that were her – and away to the horse and a gallop along an early morning forest track. But you can't gallop for long in Sussex; that is if you're not on the high downs. The mud and the rain came again; the horse stumbled and threw a shoe. A limping horse – the lanes of Wickham close, a sun that had never been visible through rain and cloud – gone – and there she was, behind him, on the horse.

'What have you done?' she screamed. 'My brothers – my brothers.'

And there they were, galloping round and round the young man's horse. But this time they didn't throw him to the ground, but reined in their horses, and the eldest brother said, 'You've shown that you'll come back for our sister; you've shown constancy – but if you truly love her, you'll put her soul to rest.'

The eldest brother then told a story. He told a story of Romani travellers passing through a Wealden forest, and of how they came upon a cache of barrels and bottles – all full of rum, brandy and fine spirits from France. Now as far as these folk were concerned, fine drink wasn't for hoarding, it was for drinking. So they drank, and they sang, and they danced, and they told stories, and they drank some more – until they all lay unconscious amidst the debris of their carousing.

It was then that the Hawkhurst Gang returned for their stash, and they were enraged by the sight that met their eyes. They fell on the unconscious Romani with cutlasses and billhooks and hacked them to pieces, after which they unceremoniously threw the remains into a ditch.

'You know that to have no words said over your earthly remains means that your soul cannot rest,' said the eldest brother. 'I will tell you where the place is, and then you can say the words, and our sister and her people can rest in peace.'

He told the young man the place, and the next day the young man found it, and he buried the bones and he said the words – and so they should all have rested in peace.

Except …

Except … the young man found the bones that were hers, and he flung them into a sack, and he galloped for home – and night fell before he reached it, and there she was sitting on the back of his horse and she screamed and threw herself into a hedgerow. He hurled himself after her, but she was gone; flitted back into the Wealden forest.

He lived for another six months – but it was six months given over to drunkenness. Some say he died of a broken heart; some say he died in a brawl in the George and Dragon Inn at Dragon's Green – maybe it was a combination of the two.

It is said, though, that if you travel through the forests of the Sussex Weald at night, you may sometimes see a flash of red between the trees; it is said that it is her, and she haunts the forest still looking for the rest of her people, and peace.

It would be good if we could find the bones, and bury them, and say the appropriate words.

THE UNQUIET GRAVE

The Wind doth blow today,
My love, a few small drops of rain;
I never had but one true-love,
In cold grave she was lain.

I'll do as much for my true-love,
As any young man may;
I'll sit and mourn all at her grave
For a twelvemonth and a day.

The twelvemonth and a day being up,
The dead began to speak:
'Oh who sits weeping on my grave,
And will not let me sleep?'

''Tis I, my love, sits on your grave,
And will not let you sleep;
For I crave one kiss of your clay-cold lips,
And that is all I seek.'

'You crave one kiss of my clay-cold lips;
But my breath smells earthy strong;
If you have one kiss of my clay-cold lips,
Your time will not be long.'

''Tis down in yonder garden green,
Love, where we used to walk,
The finest flower that ere was seen
Is withered to a stalk.'

'The stalk is withered dry, my love,
So will our hearts decay;
So make yourself content, my love,
Till Death calls you away.'

A traditional ballad; collected in Sussex.

THE GYPSUM PHARISEES

One evening I'd been telling stories in Hastings, and I decided that the next day I'd wander home through the Sussex Weald. That night I booked myself into a B&B near Brightling, and then wandered out for a pint. I got talking to a bloke at the bar, and after a random exchange of views and general setting the world to rights, we got to asking each other what we did for a living. When I say 'storyteller', people sometimes think I'm taking the mick, but this time I thought he was taking the mick, because he said he was a miner.

Well, I suppose there were the Sussex flint mines, but that was a few thousand years ago. The Weald certainly has an industrial history – it was once a major iron producing area, the smelting being fuelled by Sussex charcoal – but a twenty-first century Sussex miner?

It turned out that underneath our feet was a vast gypsum mine, gypsum being used to make plaster, plasterboard and cement. There are extensive galleries and tunnels, some big enough to drive a 4x4 through, all hidden beneath the Weald.

'You want stories?' he said. 'There's stories down there, and they're not in any book.' Coal mines are full of stories, folklore and superstitions, and the Cornish tin mines are well known for their Knockers and strange, supernatural creatures; but, apparently, in the Sussex gypsum mines there are the Pharisees.

Sometimes they can be seen trooping along in a solemn procession, but they aren't carrying gypsum; they are carrying gold. Gold torcs, bracelets, rings, helmets, headbands, bangles; and where they are taking them, nobody knows. As is usually the case with the Pharisees, they can only be seen out of the corner of the eye, so there is a hallucinogenic quality to the visual image of the little people carrying their treasure trove. Look at them straight, and they fade into the fluorescent lights and a shimmer of gold.

Well, we'd had a few drinks, and whilst I, of course, would never make up a story, I know that I can't say the same for the rest of you. He may have been making things up. But when I got home and googled Brightling, I discovered that there was a five-mile-long conveyor belt, looking similar to a centipede, which crawls across the landscape from Brightling to Mountfield, where there is a second mine. In Mountfield, in 1863, a farmer called William Butcher was ploughing his field when he found a number of yellow metal items. He thought they were brass and sold them to the local ironmongers for scrap. In fact they were gold, as the ironmonger soon discovered. Due to the law the items would have been claimed as treasure trove, so the ironmonger melted them down and sold the lot. There are only two small pieces of the Mountfield Hoard left, which can be seen in the British Museum.

Could there be a connection? I don't know, but Sussex is full of stories of buried treasure – golden calves, golden horses, treasure troves – and given all the burials of chieftains that have taken place from the Neolithic to the Saxon period, it is hardly surprising. Folklore is real; it lives and breathes. It isn't something obscure that only belongs to folklorists and antiquarians, and it isn't a conscious process. So if there are huge gypsum mines, tunnelling under the Weald, and there are people working in those mines, then there will be folklore. It won't be expressed in stories being told in art centres; it'll be expressed in informal conversations, not least a bloke talking to a stranger in a pub.

St Dunstan and the Devil

Travelling east from Brightling, up in the High Weald, we come to Mayfield. The Devil has visited Mayfield, and had as bad a time there as he did on the Downs above Brighton.

I've had cause already to remark on the industrial history of the Weald; and at one time it was a place full of the smoke and flames of iron foundries. One of the earliest ironworkers was St Dunstan; though this was purely on a hobby basis, because his day job was being an archbishop. He was a very practical saint, though, and he is the patron saint of goldsmiths. Whilst he did a certain amount of delicate, filigree stuff, just to show he was refined enough to take part in ecclesiastical affairs, he much preferred proper blacksmithing.

One evening the Devil was prowling around the Weald, thinking that this place of smoke and fire could be quite homely for a devil – if only it could be rid of the influence of the Church. Now, if St Dunstan could be corrupted, what a victory for the Antichrist! And what a great place to set up hell on earth, which, for Old Gooseberry, would be heaven on earth.

So, one day, whilst Dunstan was working in his forge, Satan turned up. Satan was well aware of the lengths the saint would go to sublimate his desires – which, unhealthily, drove him as mad with guilt as they did with lust. A baffled and bemused Beelzebub had watched Dunstan stand in a freezing furnace pond on more than one occasion; something he did in attempts to soften his ardour, reciting verses from Genesis that dwelt on the wickedness of Eve and the female responsibility for original sin.

So Satan shape-shifted into an alluring and somewhat accessible woman, and turned up at the forge whilst Dunstan was working on a particularly fine weather vane featuring silhouettes of Little Bo Peep and some rather lovely sheep.

Dunstan looked up from his work and Satan smiled – oh, what a lovely woman s/he was. Admittedly more of a man's view of what an ideal woman should look like than a real woman; but Dunstan's view of women was formed by the Old Testament, and the Devil's view of women was heavily influenced by the landlady of the Fishnet and Corset Arms, at Fishstairs-by-Sea.

'Get thee hence, thou scarlet woman,' cried the saint, as Satan made improper suggestions.

Beelzebub was clever – lewdness with accessibility, a lethal combination that St Dunstan had never before experienced. Then the Devil did what s/he considered to be a tour de force, a masterstroke – a slight opening of the robe and a flash of Ann Summers' finest (never mind the cloven hooves, for foot fetishism is very much a minority interest). But this was a miscalculation, for the saintly misogyny ran deep. Wasn't Eve as bad as the serpent? Isn't this terrible rush of desire the fault of the wicked temptress? Satan IS the temptress – and indeed Satan was. So the saint found his resolve stiffening, and he brandished his red-hot tongs and seized the Devil-woman by the nose. Satan screamed and shape-shifted into many desirable things: Churdle Pies, pond pudding, lardy cakes, goblets of huckle-my-puff; and many terrifying things: women, pub landladies, French people – but bold Dunstan hung on. At last he let go of poor Old Gooseberry's schnozzle, and the Devil leaped – in one bound – all the way to Tunbridge Wells where he plunged his nose into a spring in a cloud of steam. According to E.V. Lucas, who knows a thing or two, 'he imparted to the water its chalybeate qualities, and thus made the fortune of the town as a health resort'. So Tunbridge Wells owes its prosperity to the Great Beast, and it is very likely that those letters, signed by 'Disgusted, of Tunbridge Wells', have been sent by the Devil himself.

As for Dunstan, he had to stand in a furnace pond for three days and three nights to generally cool down, but he eventually emerged to resume his archbishopric.

Should you doubt the truth of this story, you can go to Mayfield and view the tongs for yourself; that is, if you're allowed into the girls' school where they are currently housed. As recently as 1877, Louis Jennings wrote in *Field Paths and Green Lanes in Surrey and Sussex* that he viewed the tongs at the nunnery in Mayfield.

'These are the tongs with which St. Dunstan worked his miracle,' said the worthy sister.

'I have read of the legend in my book,' said I, meaning no offence.

'It is not a legend,' replied the sister in a tone of slight reproof.

'No, no,' said I. 'I did not mean to throw any doubt upon the story.'

And quite right too; Jennings should stop being such a smart arse.

St Dunstan, as the story goes,
Once pull'd the Devil by the nose
With red-hot tongs, which made him roar,
That he was heard three miles or more. (Traditional)

NAN TUCK

If we travel from Mayfield to Uckfield, and turn left at Pound Green and Potters Green, via Limes Lane, we come to Nan Tuck's Lane. This uppity-downity lane has a bit of a ghostly reputation; and some say that Nan Tuck was a woman from Rotherfield who was suspected of murdering her husband. A Rotherfield lynch mob pursued her as she fled for the sanctuary of Buxted Church – but somewhere south of Potters Green she plunged into a coppice and was never seen again. Her shade haunts the lane, and there is a patch of ground, in a coppice, where nothing will ever grow.

There is, however, another story. This involves two young men; the sons of merchants from Uckfield, who were in a carriage, trotting towards Heathfield for a night's drinking and card-playing with friends. Ahead of them they saw a young woman, walking down the lane in the same direction. The two men elbowed each other and sniggered; both thought they could have a bit of sport. Climbing out of the carriage, they walked behind the young woman; she turned round and looked frightened, and they laughed. She walked faster, they walked faster – she clambered over a gate into a field, and they made a great show and a hullabaloo of throwing each other over the gate. They ran to catch up with her, she ran, and they ran faster – shouting at her to 'stop; stop – it's only a bit of fun'.

Then there was a tumble down shack – a rickety-rackety wooden hut – and the girl ran inside, slamming the dilapidated wooden door behind her. The laughing men pulled the door open and went inside.

'Hello, my dears,' said the withered old woman. 'My, but you're a handsome couple of fine young gentlemen and no mistake.'

'Where's the girl?' they demanded.

'Oh, you just sit down by the fire, my lovely boys, and she'll be there.'

The two men felt compelled to sit in front of the fire, and as they looked at the flames they could see flickering pictures of a young woman dancing, and an old woman stepping across the

marshes, and a baby crying, and hares boxing. The fire grew hotter, and their faces were burning; they tried to pull themselves away, but they couldn't. The fire seemed to be blazing with all the heat of a Wealden blast furnace, and their lips started to crack and their faces started to blister.

'Fly away my lovely boys,' cackled the old woman, and suddenly they were able to turn and flee – flee to the nearest pond to push their faces into the green water.

A few days later, the vengeful young men with their blistered faces returned with a lynch mob; but there was no hut – and nothing in the field to show that there had ever been anything there, except maybe that patch of ground where nothing would ever grow.

But then, Old Nan lives in Amberley Swamp, and Amberley Swamp is a long way from Nan Tuck's Lane.

THE PILTDOWN MAN

When the Weald was forest and mud, heathland and sunken lanes, there was a strange creature that lurked in the deep, dark woods – or in a thicket overlooking the ancient pathway. He can be personified in different ways, this creature. He may be the big, bad wolf; he may be the Wish Hound; the black dog; he may be a ghost, a ghoul, or a bogyman – he may even be a terrifying Willock (the *Dictionary of Sussex Dialect* tells us that a Willock is 'A wild man, one from the Weald; a wildisher. A mad man. A mad or wild (out of control) animal' ... be that as it may, he often lurked around Piltdown.

He was considered to be a mixture of creatures, a bag of differing bones – a man, a horse, a dog, a wolf. Some said that he was a friend to the charcoal burners, those smoke-blackened solitaries who lived deep in the woods. Some said that he was made from the bones of unwary travellers mixed with the remains of the inbred foresters and charcoal burners who had died deep in the forest and remained unburied, with no funerary words said over the corpses.

Now it so happens that Percy Shelley was born near here at Horsham, and the Shelley family had deep Sussex roots. Maybe Percy Shelley's wife Mary heard the story of this creature, this terrifying composite of creatures, and maybe it was this that gave her the idea for Frankenstein's monster. Should this poor, suffering creature be lurking in the Sussex Weald, rather than Switzerland or the Arctic? Possibly it was just too much for Mary Shelley to place the creature in its correct location; too close to home and reality.

Then, in 1912, came the discovery of Piltdown Man. This was exposed as a hoax in 1953, but, to be fair, most palaeontologists had considered it suspect from the beginning – though it seized the imagination of the press and the public. This skull was neatly composed to fit the naïve concept of 'the missing link'; as if evolution was a process that led simply from modern apes to modern humans, like a nineteenth-century anti-Darwinian parody of the theory.

There has been much speculation as to who was behind this hoax, but maybe all these speculations misunderstand the real purpose. Maybe the idea of providing scientific evidence was just a cover – this strange mixture of medieval human skull, orangutan jaw, and chimpanzee teeth, an attempt to create a composite creature, the beast of the wealden woods. And the creator? The Frankenstein? An inheritor of ancient and unlovely secrets.

Piltdown is now a rather desultory straggle of buildings along the A272. Sometimes, though, if you drive down that way at night, you'll see an indistinct form lurching across the road. If it turns and looks at you, and your headlights illuminate the face for just a second, it'll freeze your blood. Maybe it's Piltdown Man; maybe it's Frankenstein's monster; maybe it's the big bad wolf. Don't stick around to find out though – hurry on to Uckfield, Cuckfield, Cackle Street or Crowborough. Whatever you do, don't stop and get out of your car, or you may find that it is your bones that are next to be incorporated into the latest version of Piltdown Man.

WAGTAIL

A TALE OF TWO FORESTS, TWO SAINTS, AND AN AIRPORT

ASHDOWN FOREST

Less than forty miles from London, and only a few miles from the not-so-glamorous metropolis of Crawley, is Ashdown Forest, once known as the Forest of Anderida. There really is wild countryside close to major urban centres; a great feature of Sussex.

When we use the word 'forest' we tend to mean areas covered by trees, but its old meaning, as defined in John Manwood's *Lawes of the Forest*, first published in 1598, was 'a certain territorie of woody ground and fruitful pastures, privileged for wild beasts and fowles of the forest, chase and warren to rest and abide there, in the safe protection of the King, for his princely delight and pleasure'. In these areas there was woodland, but also heath, grassland, wetland and moorland – anywhere that supported the beasts and fowls for the hunt.

It was William the Conqueror who decreed that so much of Southern England should be designated as royal forest – and took away the rights of the inhabitants to hunt, trap and fell trees. He fully asserted his power over a vanquished country by creating an audit, Domesday Book. There is nothing like the written word to assert control.

Inevitably the inhabitants of the royal forests became law breakers, and their lives became more dangerous and marginal, though they had certain commoners' rights. As the centuries passed, and the land began to be enclosed, these rights were jealously guarded.

Ashdown Forest has the rough shape of an upside-down triangle, but has been nibbled away at the edges where large amounts of land were assigned for private enclosure and agricultural improvement – this happened in 1693 and was very much a precursor to the Enclosure Acts of the eighteenth century; though Ashdown Forest itself was spared further enclosure.

The forest hasn't always been considered beautiful – during much of its history it was a place of smoke and flame, being part of the iron industry, along with much of the rest of the Weald. Then in 1822 William Cobbett described it as 'a heath, with here and there a few birch scrubs upon it, verily the most villainously ugly spot I ever saw in England'; though to be fair, at that time Crawley was just a village, and ugly hadn't become an art form.

Pat Bowen has written, in *20 Sussex Walks* (a book of walks with considerably greater depth than the usual collection):

Waymarkers or signposts are not permitted within the boundaries of Ashdown Forest (such is the decree of the Board of Conservators) which means that when planning to walk there it is best to allow time for losing the path and finding it (or another one). The challenge is increased because the boundaries of the open access land have no logic – there are large and small enclosures of private land dotted about, the result of ancient squatting successes, encroachments, aristocratic emparkments and other accidents of history. But the rewards make it all worthwhile: they include wide open spaces on high ridges, deep valleys with shady streams, ancient woodlands, rare and unusual plants, intriguing features and historical associations to explore.

So I love to walk these woods, valleys and villainous heaths, because I relish losing the path and finding another; I relish being confused by the seemingly illogical, because, as Pat points out, the rewards make it all worthwhile. Which leads me to a story; something that happened to me when I was wandering Ashdown Forest with my tent and a week to spare.

Wildisher's Castle

One evening during this wander, I'd stopped, put up my tent, baked some spuds over a fire, and was just enjoying a can of beer when I heard a 'clink-clink-clink', and out of the darkness came the strangest-looking man I'd ever seen.

He was a big man, with long raggedy hair that stuck out in all directions, and a big beard. He was dressed in raggedy clothes that looked like they were made out of sacking, and on his back he had a pack made out of wood and sailcloth, from which hung the pots, kettles and pans that were 'clink-clinking' together. I found this a somewhat alarming sight as I sat alone by a fire, with evening turning to night.

He stood on the other side of the fire, regarding me through the smoke.

'Can you spare a passing traveller a drink?' he asked in a rough voice that sounded more like a command than a polite request.

Nervously I handed him one of my tinnies, and he sat down opposite me examining it curiously, testing the tin with his fingers. After a while it became apparent that he didn't know how to open it; it was as if he came from another time when beer wouldn't have come in cans, only bottles and barrels. I took the can and opened it for him. He took a swig, and then said, 'I'm Tom Tinker, and I'm a tinkerman.'

I was stuck for words – he was like someone from centuries ago, and he certainly didn't have the smooth hands and modern complexion of a re-enactor. He took some thoughtful swigs from the can, before saying, 'Have you ever heard tell of Wildisher's Castle?' I confessed I hadn't, and he proceeded to tell me a story.

'One winter's night I'd been selling my pots and kettles in the village of Wych Cross, for there they make everything out of iron, and they love their iron cannons which they're as happy to sell to the French or Spanish as the English; but they still need the tin mugs and pots. I was heading into the forest when it started to snow, and it came down thick and fast. I knew I had to take shelter, or I'd likely freeze to death, and the only place nearby was Wildisher's Castle, so Wildisher's Castle it was. Now, it ent really a castle, just an old tumble down ruin where some Wealden wildishers lived a long time ago, and I came up to the big door and hauled it open. Inside was a room with a stone bench down the one side, a stone bench down the other, and at the far end of the room a big fireplace. Who should be sitting on the benches but a whole host of they bloody Pharisees – and as I went in they set up a-howling and a-shouting.

'"Get back out into the bloody snow," they shouted, but I'm Tom Tinker, and I'm frightened of nothing. "You get out in the bloody snow and get shrammed," I roared, and chased them all out with my pudding-lifter. I ent frightened of they Pharisees – I'm a tinkerman, and I sees them by many a Pook's Lane, and they can't put no chuckle-headed curse on me, the stuggy little twaddling shoolers.

'I lit a fire in the grate, boiled up the water in my kettle, and made myself a mug of tea – just what I needed on a cold winter's night. I was about to drink the tea, when out of the corner of my eye I saw something move. The door handle was slowly turning. Then the door creaked open, and in came the most 'orrible Willock you've ever seen. He had sharp terrible pointy teeth. How many teeth do you think he had?'

Now, I hate it when people do that – ask a question that is impossible to answer – and then stare at you, challenging you for a reply.

'I don't know,' I replied.

'Go on, you tell I,' Tom demanded, irritatingly.

'I dunno – um – seven?'

'Course it was,' he said, bafflingly.

'Seven sharp pointy teeth he had – a long, warty, twitchy nose, gurt big, round, staring yellow eyes like saucers, and a long pointy tail. He came in and sat down opposite I, staring at me all the while.

'"GIVE US A MUG OF TEA, TOM TINKER,' he roared.So I poured him out a mug of tea and passed it over to him. He just snatched it, swigged it up in one, scrunched up the mug, and hurled it back at me. But I'm Tom Tinker, and I'm frightened of nothing. Quick as a flash I picked up one of my frying pans and whacked it back again (that's how cricket was invented; you don't want to believe that rubbish about it coming from Hampshire). It hit him on the head, he gave a gurt howl, and ran out the door.

'"Well, I dunno," thought I, "I'm going to have to make another mug of tea."

'So I boiled up the kettle again, and poured out another mug of tea. Slowly – slowly – the door handle was turning, and – creeeeeak – the door was opening. And what do you think came in?'

I knew he wasn't going to take 'dunno' for an answer.

'Another Willock?' I suggested.

'That's roight – but this one was bigger and uglier than the last one – and this one had TWO HEADS (and fourteen sharp, pointy teeth). He came in, sat down opposite me, and roared out, "GIVE US TWO MUGS OF TEA, TOM TINKER!"'

I began to detect a pattern.

'So I filled up two mugs, handed them to him, he snatched them, swigged them up, ONE, TWO, and hurled 'em back at me, ONE, TWO. But I'm Tom Tinker, and I'm frightened of nothing. Quick as a flash, I picked up a frying pan, and whacked 'em back (this is how tennis was invented). They hit the Willock on the two heads, ONE TWO – and he howled and ran out the door. "Oh my Lord," sez I to myself, "I'm going to have to make another mug of tea". So I boiled up the kettle again, poured out another mug of tea, when out of the corner of my eye I saw something move. Slowly, slowly, the door handle was turning – and creeeeeeeaak, the door started to open. And what do you think came in?'

'Another Willock?' I replied, somewhat warily.

'And how many heads did he have?'

'Three?'

'That's roight. And how many round staring yellow eyes?'

'Six?'

'That's roight. And how many sharp, pointy teeth?'

'Um – er …'

'You'm roight slow at the adding up, you couldn't sell no pots and kettles – den and half a one-erum; twenty-one, you gurt blumber brain.

'Well the Willock came in, sat down opposite me, and with no pleases or thank yous, roared out, "GIVE US THREE MUGS OF TEA, TOM TINKER." So I poured out three mugs of tea, handed 'em to the Willock; he snatched 'em, ONE TWO THREE, swigged 'em up, ONE TWO THREE, scrunched 'em up in his claws and hurled 'em back at me. But I'm Tom Tinker, and I'm frightened of nothing – so quick as a flash I picked up a frying pan and knocked 'em back again, ONE TWO THREE – and what did he do?'

'Scream and run out the door?' I suggested.

'No,' said Tom, eyeing me triumphantly, 'that he did not. This time he stood up, and started to walk towards me; "I'M GOING TO GET YOU FOR THAT, TOM TINKER" he roared. Well, I looked round – the fire was just in the middle of the fireplace, so I got in beside it and scrambled up the chimney. Scritch-scratch-scritch-scratch – the Willock scrambled up behind me. So I climbed out of the chimney and ran across the roof, but splish-splosh, splish-splosh through the snow, the Willock came after me. So I climbed down the outside of Wildisher's Castle, and scritch-scratch-scritch-scratch – the Willock came climbing down after me. So I ran back in the door, with the Willock right behind me; I could feel his breath on the back of my neck. The first thing I saw was the end of the Willock's long, green, scaly tail sticking out of the fireplace. So I grabbed it, waved it in front of its face (the middle one), as it came through the door, and it opened its mouth and bit its own tail. Chomp-chomp-chomp – all the way up its own tail, till it sank its sharp, pointy teeth into its own arse. It whirled around fifteen times like a Catherine Wheel, gave a great howl, and ran off into the forest.

'"Well, I dunno," said I, "I'm going to have to make another mug of tea." So I picked up the kettle again – poured myself some tea and …'

'Four heads?' I said wearily.

'No, this time I drank my tea and stayed the night in Wildisher's Castle. But whatever you do, nipper, don't you ever spend the night in Wildisher's Castle.'

'Don't worry, I won't,' I said, as Tom Tinker polished off the beer.

'Thank you for the beer,' he said, and off he went. The last I saw of him he was disappearing into the darkness on that old Wealden track, and the last I heard was the clink-clink-clink of the pots and kettles fading into the forest. Well, I was tired, so I got up, piddled into the fire because I like to watch the steam rise, climbed into my sleeping bag, and went to sleep.

Now, this was in the early 1990s, before mobile phones, so it wasn't till I got to Fairwarp the next day that I phoned home from a telephone box (remember them?) and told my children the story. They didn't believe me; they said I was telling a load of old porky pies. This upset me deeply – because I'm certain Tom Tinker wouldn't lie to me, and I'm sure you know that I wouldn't lie to you.

> I've finished my true story,
> So now I'm off to bed,
> And if you didn't believe me,
> You can go and boil your head.

St Leonard's Forest

Travelling east from Ashdown Forest we come to St Leonard's Forest, which is a Cinderella amongst forests. I say this because I think that it is underappreciated. A drive there from Ashdown Forest can take you past Weir Wood Reservoir and Ardingly Reservoir, where the scenery is almost like that of north Wales or Scotland; something I find astonishingly unexpected so close to Crawley and Gatwick airport: runways, motorways, roundabouts, link roads and urban sprawl. This forest, unlike Ashdown Forest, has a certain dark and gloomy quality, which isn't reminiscent of Cinderella; more of her wicked stepmother.

St Leonard's Forest is a forest where you can get lost. Recently I parked my car by the side of the road there – without thinking to note what road it was – and wandered into the forest without a map, just intending to take a short walk. As usual, I went further than intended, because every incline, every twist and turn in the path, beckoned 'just a little further'. It was winter and it got dark quickly and early, and I got hopelessly lost. I found myself gazing out at slopes of dark, Germanic pine forest, all lit by a raggedy moon. There was quite a feeling of malevolence about the woods, and if I was 'pixie-led', that phrase that describes being led astray by the other people, then these pixies were more like little devils.

When eventually I came across a road, I had absolutely no idea where my car was, or what road I'd parked it on. In the postscript to this book I will sing the praises of serendipity – of the aimless wander; the opportunity to come across unexpected wonders – but don't be as daft as me; show a little common sense!

St Leonard the Dragon Slayer

Æthelweard's Chronicle of AD 770 mentions that 'Monstrous serpents were seen in the country of the Southern Angles that is called Sussex', and it was up to St Leonard to get rid of them. He crossed from France on a millstone, and decided to convert the Sussexonians to Christianity. Sussex folk have a reputation for obstinacy; 'we wunt be druv' (we won't be pushed around) is the unofficial county motto. The good saint's efforts at evangelising the folk who lived on the flat land between the sea and the South Downs were proving unsuccessful, so he pretty much got the hump and thought he'd go somewhere really quiet and remote and lead a meditative life. He crossed the high downs, and, in the Weald, he saw a vast forest, ideal for sitting in and contemplating all sorts of meaningful stuff. In the depths of that forest he built a hermitage, and settled down to a quiet life of meditation. His meditations, though, were disturbed. Firstly it was those irritating nightingales. It wasn't just that they were noisy; it was that their song sounded so sensuous. St Leonard really wanted strictness and discomfort, and that nightingale song punctured his comfortable discomfort.

Things got worse though. People started to hammer on his door; 'Knucker, knucker,' they shouted. 'You're a man of God, save us from the knuckers.'

What had happened was that a knucker had emerged from one of the many knucker holes that were then to be found in the flat land between the sea and the Downs, the area which St Leonard had so much difficulty evangelising. This knucker had wandered over the South Downs and found itself lost in the Weald. Knuckers are not known for their intelligence, and their senses of geography and direction are notoriously hopeless, so it was unable to find its way home. In the forest the knucker had no other knucker to mate with, and so it resorted to binary fission, or asexual reproduction; an unusual ability for a creature so large, but then knuckers are unusual creatures. The result was that the forest was soon infested with genetically identical knuckers, and they took to eating Wildishers, and even the Willocky Wealden woodland beasties the Wildishers were so fond of making.

St Leonard had had enough. His head rattled by nightingale song and folk shouting about knuckers, he stormed out of his hermitage and started laying into the surprised knuckers with stave, cross, and ropes with Shepherd's Crowns (a type of fossil often found in Sussex) tied to the ends. Every time he killed a knucker, however, one particular knucker grew larger.

Finally all the knuckers were slain – except for the remaining gigantic monster. A huge battle ensued. St Leonard used both violence and the power of the Word – his incantations were a force unto themselves. Finally the monster lay dead, and a victorious but injured St Leonard crawled back to his hermitage. Where his blood stained the ground grew lilies of the valley, and there is still a part of the forest known as 'The Lily Beds'.

God spake unto St Leonard and asked what he'd like as a reward, and St Leonard saith unto God, 'Please Lord, rid the forest of snakes, so that I can be as good as St Patrick, and, please, shut those bloody nightingales up.' God then rid the forest of nightingales, because it was St Leonard's devotions unto God that they were disturbing, but He didn't rid the forest of snakes, because St Leonard's motivation was clearly based on unworthy envy. Grass snakes and occasional adders can still be found in the woods – and it may be that some of those knuckers survived, because the story doesn't end there.

THE CONTINUOUS SURVIVAL OF THE FOREST KNUCKERS

According to *The Harleian Miscellany*, a seventeenth-century compendium of bits and pieces collated and edited by Samuel Johnson, there was a monster in the woods. This is described in 'A Discourse relating a strange and monstrous Serpent (or Dragon) lately discovered, and yet living, to the great Annoyance and divers Slaughters both of Men and Cattell, by his strong and violent Poyson: In Sussex, two Miles from Horsam, in a Woode called St Leonard's Forrest, and thirtie Miles from London, this present Month of August, 1614. With the true Generation of Serpents.' This discourse tells us that in St Leonard's Forest, 'a vast and unfrequented place, heathie, vaultie, full of unwholesome shades, and over-growne hollowes', there dwells a terrible serpent, or maybe enormous slug would be a better description, for it left 'a glutinous and slimie matter' behind it, like a slug or snail trail. It is shaped like the axle of a cart, thicker in the middle than the ends, and is 9ft or more in length. When it encounters people or cattle, it raises its head upright, and looks about 'with great arrogancy', before flooring its victim with its vile and noisome breath.

This story must be true, because John Steele, Christopher Holder and a widow woman dwelling near Faygate were willing to sign a piece of paper saying they'd encountered the serpent. Others also certified the truth of all that has been here related, such as 'the carrier of Horsam, who lieth at the White Horse in Southwarke', and surely no one could doubt the word of someone who 'lieth at the White Horse in Southwarke'.

Nearly two centuries later, however, there was someone who acted as a protector to these knuckers, and maybe that was because she felt as rejected and shunned as these unfortunate creatures. Her name was Halima, though it had been both Frenchified to Helene, and Anglicised to Helena. She had come from India, as the wife of Colonel de Boigne, a French military adventurer and mercenary. She was the daughter of a colonel in the Persian Guard of the Great Moghul; though she was really more Indian than Persian in upbringing. De Boigne, a regular charmer, abandoned her for a sixteen-year-old French girl called Adele – though it has to be said that his marriage to Adele didn't last long.

Halima retreated into the depths of St Leonard's Forest, where she lived alone.

In India she had watched snake charmers – something that had more to do with her French husband's taste for the 'exotic' than it had to do with her normal Indian life. Now, however, living alone in the woods, she came across the last of the knuckers; genetically weakened by centuries of binary fission, and no longer able to reproduce. The knucker danced for her, and she played music that echoed through the forest and replaced the lost song of the nightingales in its sweetness.

When Halima died she was buried in the Anglican graveyard in Horsham, but with her grave facing Mecca. What happened to the knucker when it died I don't know; maybe there still are knuckers in the forest.

> The Knucker lived in the wood on the hill,
> And if it's not gone, it lives there still.

THE CRAWLEY-CRAWLEY CREATURE.

You may be lost in the remoteness of St Leonard's Forest, you may hear tawny owls call to each other, or the sound of a shrew being murdered by a fox or an owl, but at the same time you will be hearing, above you, the sound of airliners going into reverse thrust as they decelerate into Gatwick Airport. A reminder of how close all this antithesis to the forest is. You may be further south, up on the high downs on a sunny day, and see a vapour trail in the sky; Roger Deakin has remarked that it is 'strange how beautiful such sky-litter can be'. You may wonder where that plane is heading for; a wistful feeling, a dream of faraway places – even though someone, faraway, will be dreaming of Sussex.

Gatwick is the UK's second largest airport, and has the world's busiest single-use runway. Gatwick is actually Anglo-Saxon for goat farm, but things look a little different now. Planes, runways, airport terminals – is this the stuff of folklore?

Of course it is.

When planes fly into Gatwick they sometimes carry hitch-hikers, stowaways in the hold, or creatures and organisms that can survive the cold and the lack of oxygen. Or at least, they do in stories. In this serpent-storied part of Sussex, modern legends have added themselves to the old tales.

Three Bridges is an area of Crawley, and it is in Three Bridges that I heard the tale; it is a folk story because I have heard slightly varying versions of it from children in different schools, though who knows how the story originated.

In an alley between takeaways there was a bin. The detritus from the takeaways was thrown into the bin, and inside there was something that fed on the scraps and leftovers; something that crawled from Gatwick Airport through pipes and drains and concrete culverts; something that found rich pickings in a land where food is thrown away. All it had to do was eat and grow, eat and grow, until it grew too big for the bin.

Its appetite was now degraded by its diet of takeaway leftovers, and it developed a more sinister, debased appetite. Given that many of the children of Crawley lived on a similar diet, the creature found these fatty, toxic beings to be a perfect delicacy. So sometimes, when a child is going to school late because they can't be bothered to get up on time, and it isn't considered important in their home, or maybe when a child doesn't go to school at all, but hangs around

the shopping precinct or the park, then the creature will pounce and there'll be a squealing and a slurping of blood.

The creature is believed to live somewhere around St Leonard's Forest – it feels at home there amidst ancient memories of serpents and knuckers. Its hunting ground, though, is Crawley, and its prey is kids that live on junk food.

If teachers were to tell such a story it would be considered appalling, and they'd probably end up on a disciplinary. Maybe that's why it has to be the children themselves who come up with such stories!

The Travels of St Cuthman and his Mum

The forest was named after St Leonard, but there was another saint who paid a visit.

St Cuthman came from far distant Chidham, down on the coast near Bosham. Cuthman's father had been a merchant, trading out of Bosham, and when the Vikings were spotted sailing around Selsey Bill towards Bosham, it was just too much for Cuthman's father to leave his goods to these barbarians and flee to the hills with the rest of the population. In trying to protect his goods he lost his life, leaving Cuthman, his only child, to look after his infirm and ailing wife.

The Vikings had taken everything, including the largest church bell, and it was their just rewards that they should all sink to the bottom of the sea; but they also took the valuables of Bosham with them. So Cuthman and his mother were left with nothing, and Cuthman eked out a living as a shepherd, and struggled to care for his ailing mother.

But Cuthman was a pious lad, and the solitary life of a shepherd enabled him to talk to God. He would draw an imaginary circle on the ground, and his small flock of sheep would remain safely within that circle. Cuthman would then kneel upon a stone – he called it the kneeling stone, and maybe it is still there near Chidham – and he would pray to God. It was during one of these contemplative moments that God spoke to Cuthman.

'Travel north and east,' said the Lord, 'till you come to the dark forest wherein dwelt my disciple, Leonard. Continue the work of Leonard and build a church; for within that dark and unwholesome place, many of the populace are still heathen Wildishers, and you must bring the word of God to them.'

Now, many a saint would have left everyone and everything to do this, for the word of God seems so much more important than mere personal relationships to the purist – but Cuthman was by necessity a practical young man, and he saw the word of God as more than voices heard during contemplation; and being a humane sort of fellow, he knew he could never abandon his old mum.

So Cuthman built a wheelbarrow, and the barrow had a rope halter which he put around his neck as he proceeded to trudge through the Sussex mud and up to the high chalk downs, with his old mother seated in the wheelbarrow in stately fashion.

Many days later, a weary Cuthman looked down at the great Wealden forest and saw a plume of smoke rising up above the tiny settlement of Warninglid. He trudged along Spronkett's Lane, his old mum bouncing along in the barrow in front of him, and into Earwig Lane. Finally the rope halter could take no more – it snapped, dumping Cuthman's mum unceremoniously into the Sussex mud. There were some peasants in a nearby field, and they all started to laugh.

'Funny?' shouted Cuthman. 'You buggers (sorry, Lord) need to get your sense of humour looked at.' Cuthman's poor old mum just grumbled, 'Bloody mud, bloody missions, bloody wheelbarrow.'

Cuthman then proceeded to fashion a new halter out of elder branches. This made the peasants laugh even more.

'Lummox, nodbucket, spronkett noggin, selig, madbrain mawkin,' they jeered, waving their scythes in a derisive manner.

'Men mock and heaven shall weep,' cursed Cuthman in a very authoritative tone, and the heavens opened; but only over that particular field, ruining the crop.

Now, elder is often associated with witches and wickedness and Elynge Ellet; but this time the elder was given holy strength, and it could even support the good saint's mum.

She, however, shouted, 'I am not going any further into this horrible forest – turn about, son, and head back south if you know what's good for you.'

'Mother,' quoth the saint, 'the Almighty has instructed me.'

'I'm as almighty as you'll bloody find,' she replied. 'Turn around, or I'll fetch you one round the ear.'

Cuthman was a wise saint, and since God didn't seem to be saying anything directly, he reasoned that God might well be speaking through his mother; so he turned round and headed south again.

It wasn't till he came to a settlement wherein dwelt a heathen people calling themselves the People of the Stones, that the elder halter broke, once again pitching Cuthman's mother onto her backside.

'I'm not going any bloody further,' she announced – and so they didn't. Cuthman converted the locals, and they built a wooden church in the settlement of the People of the Stones; all at the foot of Chanklebury. The settlement became known as Steyning, and Cuthman was, and is, its patron saint.

However, to this day, in the Weald near St Leonard's Forest, and next to Earwig Lane, there are often strange, localised downpours. Then, the earwigs will crawl out from the mossy banks, and get inside your shirt and your underclothes. It is easy then to understand just how Cuthman's mother got so grumpy.

Dragon's Green

It seems appropriate to conclude a chapter full of dragons and knuckers at the hamlet of Dragon's Green, south-west of St Leonard's Forest. It is sometimes said that this hamlet got its name from the last of the St Leonard's Forest dragons, and given that the excellent pub is called the George and Dragon, the Dutch anglophile Pieter Boogaart is prompted to comment, 'I suppose the question of why this pub is not called the Leonard and Dragon must be considered as foolish and foreign …'

However, as Boogaart points out, the name of the village probably originates from a surname: Dragon. Or maybe the operative word is Green, and not dragon at all; for Dragon's Green and Green Street were once a straggling hamlet until, in the nineteenth century, they were cut in two by the construction of the new turnpike road. It was Egbyrt Green, from around here, who travelled all the way to Hampshire to slay the Wherwell cockatrice, a story that is told by that renowned folklorist Michael O'Leary in his *Folk Tales of Hampshire and Isle of Wight*. The story I want to recount now, however, is more recent, and really does carry a lot of pathos.

Out at the front of the George and Dragon there is a large stone cross, of the sort to be found in a churchyard, not a pub garden. The cross bears the following inscription: 'In loving memory of Walter the Albino son of Alfred and Charlotte Budd. Born February 12th 1867. Died February 18th 1893. May God forgive those who forgot their duty to him who was just and afflicted.'

Walter Budd was the son of the proprietors of the George and Dragon at the end of the nineteenth century. Because of his albinism and epilepsy he was taunted and bullied; and when he was accused of theft this was the final humiliation, and he drowned himself.

His parents put the cross over his grave in the churchyard, but the vicar and some of the parishioners objected to the final sentence of the inscription, and demanded that the cross be removed. So Walter's righteously angry parents re-erected the cross in the pub garden, and it stands there still – a lesson and a warning about the destructive power of bullying. William Budd knew what it was like to be treated as an outsider.

SQUARING
THE CIRCLE

Once upon a time, the inside of an English church was a riot of colour and pictorial storytelling. The pictures would tell Bible stories, legends of saints, and local tales – and no doubt a mixture of all these. They were a physical representation of the way stories and myth melt, merge and grow; they were extraordinarily rich. It is sometimes said that they were there because the congregations were illiterate; as if this was somehow an inferior way of accessing information than through the written word. It seems to me that this is to 'deify' cold print, something which is simply a technique; and it is to fail to recognise the extraordinary complexity of people's belief and inner life represented in these skilful acts of devotion. This was all belittled by the arrogance of the Reformation when, in a terrible act of national vandalism, these paintings were whitewashed over.

Every so often fragments of this graphic storytelling are uncovered, and, in 1868, a fragment was uncovered in Wisborough Green Church.

It dates from the thirteenth century and appears to show St James of Compostela. St James is the patron saint of pilgrims, and the pilgrimage to Santiago de Compostela in southern Spain has for centuries been one of the most well-known pilgrimages in Europe – now so popular it has become positively trendy!

The A272 – A Pilgrim's Way

Wisborough Green is on the A272, and Pieter Boogaart has written a glorious book about this road. Boogaart hypothesises that this is a pilgrimage route, linking the great ecclesiastical centres of Winchester and Canterbury. The pilgrims may not have actually called it the A272, but it follows the old way.

Boogaart asks what the evidence for this hypothesis is, and replies to himself:

> Scant, really, I'll tell you what I have so far:
> In the middle ages a popular name for inns along pilgrim ways was The Angel. Both Midhurst and Petworth have Angel hotels. They are not medieval hotels, but it's impossible to say how old their names are. Traditions die hard. The names may have survived even if the buildings haven't. And having two cases seems more than coincidental. Let's say that it's something.

Oh, I do like the idea of the survival of names, especially now that so many pubs are taken over by trendy young philistines who throw the old names away and replace them with advertising slogans.

Boogaart's second piece of evidence is the mural in Wisborough Green; his third a description of the Bull Inn in Newick as a resting place for pilgrims; and his fourth a description of Uckfield that says it lies on one of the variants of the Winchester to Canterbury pilgrims' route.

Of course Sussex can supply all sorts of variants to this route. There could be the high and open spaces of the Downs – now the South Downs Way; there could be well-trodden paths through the Weald. I like the thought of the A272 as a pilgrims' way, though. It is a road that runs through Sussex like a story: through Cross-in-Hand and Pond Green, through Piltdown – and beware of Piltdown Man lurching across the road – it fringes Ashdown and St Leonard's Forests, nudges in between Dragon's Green and Shipley, through Billingshurst, Petworth and Midhurst, before tumbling into Hampshire through Trotton and Rogate and across the border into Sheet.

The road is a story, and the story is a road.

THE AMBERSHAM TIME SHIFT

South Ambersham is only just off the A272, near Midhurst. It is a good few miles from Hampshire, but it used to contain a little slice of Hampshire. This was a strangely detached part of the county, which was absorbed into Sussex with a parliamentary act – the Counties (Detached Parts) Act of 1844. However, when that slice of Hampshire became Sussex, North Ambersham vanished. How can there be a South Ambersham without a North Ambersham?

In North Ambersham there was an enigmatic standing stone called the Hegstone. Now, this could have been a hedgestone – a standing stone in a hedge, sometimes a boundary marker; or perhaps some larger version of a 'hagstone', or a holed stone that was hung in barns in Hampshire and Sussex to ward off bad luck and drive away evil spirits and ill-intentioned Pharisees.

However, North Ambersham – hegstone, dwellings and all – vanished; it was as if it had never been there.

Yet in Hampshire, just north of the port of Hampton, the port that took the name Southampton, a riverside settlement appeared. It was called Northam – and if you look on the old maps you will see something down by the river called 'The Hegstone'. It is written in the antique script that denotes an ancient monument – but its appearance was sudden, as was its subsequent disappearance.

Northam is, of course, North Ambersham – for if Sussex was going to claim a slice of Hampshire, Hampshire was going to grab a slice of Sussex. Northam is now part of Southampton's inner city, and most of its inhabitants have no idea that it was spirited away from rural Sussex. However, if you go to Northam, and wander down to the River Itchen between scrapyards and warehouses, you might suddenly feel a flash of awareness – and feel the time and place shift. On the other hand, you might not.

There is still a strange quality to the area around South Ambersham. That is surely why, in 1975, an episode of *Doctor Who* called 'Terror of the Zygons' was filmed on Ambersham Common. The setting was supposed to represent a Scottish moor; but time, place and space can shift around South Ambersham, as it does around Ambersham Common, Ambersham Hollow Road and the nearby Three Moles public house.

THE CURFEW GARDENS AND A DISCOURSE UPON BELLS

The Ambersham area has always had the capacity to 'pixie-lead' unwary travellers, whether or not they've had a few in the Three Moles.

There was once a traveller, who, on a dark and stormy night, found himself lost amidst the woods and heaths around Ambersham, after he'd managed to stray from the Midhurst road. To be cold is one thing, but to be wet and cold is another, and he was soaked to the skin. His disorientation caused him to panic, and he'd fallen several times and was plastered with mud.

Then, through the howling of the wind, the creaking of the trees, and the sound of pouring, lashing rain, he heard a more comforting sound – the tolling of a bell.

That feeling of civilisation, of people nearby, of the possibility of warmth, drew him and he followed the sound of the bell. It was hard to see far in the tempest, but suddenly Midhurst was in front of him – and the curfew bell was still tolling.

He was so grateful that he gave a quarter of an acre of land in Knockhundred Row to the town, and called it Curfew Gardens. The income from this land pays for a ringer to toll the bell, for the bell to be repaired when necessary, and for the maintenance of the tower and belfry. The bell rings the curfew to this day.

The story of the traveller who finds his way to safety by following the sound of a bell occurs throughout England –

but only in Midhurst does the curfew bell still ring to explain the story – so plainly this is the true one!

Bells ring throughout the old tales. We have already encountered the Bosham bell, but also at Slinfold, not so very far east from Midhurst, there is a story of a great bell that was made in Rome, which was dropped from the Alfoldean Bridge into a bog next to the River Arun. A team of white oxen were unable to haul it out, and when the Time Team assisted in the excavation of the Romano-British site there, I don't believe they found it either! The same story is told of Etchingham in East Sussex, where a bell was dropped into a moat. This is a story that pops up throughout England, from Knowlton in Dorset to the distant, northern wilds of Cheshire. As a team of white oxen attempt to haul the bell out of the lake/river/bog, it is blasphemy that causes the chain to snap:

> We have now got the Slindon Bell
> In spite of all the Devils in hell

says one of the men (substitute whichever location for Slindon), and SNAP – the chain breaks and the bell sinks back into the deep.

But, as Westwood and Simpson write: 'Church bells were essential for communal life. They rang for weddings, deaths and funerals; for national and local celebrations; to announce the times of service, and in some places, as a sunset curfew.' In medieval times a bell was baptised, and its tolling could drive away devils and thunderstorms.

So, like the call of the muezzin in many an Islamic country, or the call to prayer from a Sikh gurdwara in the Punjab, the sound of church bells ringing across the woods and meadows is central to the English story; and central to the country's folklore.

The Mercer's Son of Midhurst

Once upon a time there was, in Midhurst, a rich mercer, a cloth merchant, and he had business dealings with a clothier from Guildford in Surrey. Now the mercer had a son, and the clothier had a daughter – and didn't the mercer's son make a big issue about falling in love with the clothier's daughter.

> He cryed night and day,
> Alack I dye for love.
> Alack I dye for love,
> Beauty disdaineth me.

Now, falling in love is one thing, but falling in love with a girl from Surrey is another – it's bound to hit the pocket as well as the heart – and when that girl is a clothier's daughter, well, it's a double whammy of sartorial obsession.

'Fair Phillis, pity me,' cried the young man to the rather bored young woman. 'Fair Venus silver Dove, fair Phillis, pity me.'

And the unfortunate mercer had to put up with this too.

'Oh father, father, she has stolen my heart, I can but weep.'

'Bloody hell,' thought the mercer, 'he's like his mum, all tears and oh woe, and foll-di-roll. When she kicked the bucket, I mean, passed away, I thought I'd get some peace. Why can't he fall in love with the butcher's daughter; a fine, lovely great lump of a girl – it was her mum I should have married all those years ago – but, no, I had to go for "refinement", and now what's he winging on about? He's fallen for a trollop from Surrey.'

As for the clothier's daughter, she was less than impressed by this young man who kept insisting on reading her poetry.

'You can have the loftiest mind in Christendom,' she said to him, 'but that won't bring home the bacon.'

> Now, if we were to be wed;
> Where goods and wealth is small,
> Want causeth deadly strife.

Ah, she was a philosopher, and the conclusion to her philosophising was 'Goods increaseth love'.

The young man, in between tears and love-struck sighs, mused upon this. She had made it plain that before there could be any 'tumbling in her lap' there should be a certain amount of gold tumbling in her lap – and so he went to his father with pleas and entreaties: 'Father, wilt thou bestow upon me …?'

'How much…?'

'More …'

'How much …'

'All … the money … the house … the land … the business.'

So the young man travelled to Guildford and went down on bended knee – and the fair Phillis said 'Yes', and the father conveyed all he had to his son.

'My dearest son,' he said, 'now you own everything – you must be good to me.'

Truth be told, the father was looking forward to a life of leisure; like King Lear he thought he could shrug off all responsibility and be looked after by a dutiful son and daughter-in-law.

But after the wedding, the old father was just a bit of a nuisance, and his proportion of everything – food, drink, clothing, shelter – became less and less; till eventually he was thrown out onto the street. The young man's feelings of love soon lost their poetry, and he became a hard-bargaining mercer; the young woman found little comfort in the wealth she had so desired, and so none of them lived happily ever after.

Oh dear – well don't blame me, dear reader, I didn't dream the story up. It comes from a traditional ballad called: 'An excellent ballad of the mercer's son of Midhurst, and the cloathier's daughter of Guilford' to the tune of 'Dainty come thou to me'. According to William E.A. Axon, writing in *Bygone Sussex* in 1897: 'The moral of the story is that parents should not during life relinquish the power over their property and transfer it to their children; or else they may expect an ungrateful return.' (He adds: 'If an old house at Midhurst or at Guildford has not yet been consecrated by tradition to the Mercer of Midhurst, or to the Clothier of Guildford, it is easy still to remedy the defect. "Nothing so easy as to make a tradition," says Sir Walter Scott.' What a terribly cynical conclusion both Mr Axon and Sir Walter arrive at with regard to tradition!)

As far as I'm concerned, the moral of the story should be, 'Watch out for those Surrey girls, and if your son fancies one, keep a tight hold on your wallet.'

THE ETERNAL WANDERINGS OF A FRATRICIDE

North of Midhurst, somewhere near the village of Lurgashall, there was once a grand house, and in that house there lived two brothers, Thomas and Tankerville Lewknor.

It was Thomas who courted a young woman from the neighbouring Fitzmaurice family; and a date was set for the wedding.

But Tankerville had also fallen in love with the young woman, and he lured her away from Thomas. She broke off the engagement, and fell into the arms of Tankerville.

So Thomas took a knife and he stabbed his brother through the heart. The full horror of his actions fell upon him, and he fled through Windfallwood and Coochway and Hobstevens, stumbling through the undergrowth, until deep in the woods he came upon a hermitage.

'Tell me what troubles you,' said the hermit. 'With God's good grace I can absolve you of your sins.'

'No one can absolve me of this sin,' cried Thomas.

'Tell me,' said the hermit, 'God can forgive.'

So Thomas told the hermit, and the hermit gaped in horror.

'Fratricide!' he shouted. 'Fratricide; the mark of Cain is upon you. I have not the means to find forgiveness for such a crime.'

'What can I do?' wailed Thomas.

'Go south – keep going south – go south,' said the hermit.

So Thomas went south and two magpies went with him, one on the left and one on the right, with their harsh cries and juddering flight. He stumbled over Halfway Bridge, through Ambersham Common, over the Downs and Bow Hill, down through Kingley Vale, until he reached the port of Bosham. As he passed through the town it was silent and empty, but at the quay there was a ship, a three-masted carrack. The magpies flew aboard and one became a grey-bearded captain, and the other the first mate.

'Come aboard, come aboard,' they called in their rough, magpie voices, and Thomas clambered onto the ship.

An invisible crew cast off, and hoisted the sails, and they sailed through Chichester Harbour, and out into the channel. They sailed over the Mixon Hole, past the Isle of Wight, the Cap de la Hague and Sark, then west along the north coast of Brittany. As they did so the weather grew dark and threatening, and St Elmo's Fire flickered around the masts and yards of the ship. To this day tales are told in Brittany of the ghost ship that sailed the north coast, flickering with uncanny blue lightning until she disappeared beyond Finisterre, the world's end, and out into the wide Atlantic.

Always the storm threatened, but never arrived. The horizon rumbled with distant thunder, and crackled with lightning, as a steady wind drove the ship southwards. Down through the Atlantic she sailed – league after league – till she crossed the equator, and still she sailed south. Finally, with a howling wind and freezing sea spray, and with the Cape of Good Hope away to the port, and Cape Horn away to the starboard, she changed course and beat her way westwards; towards the Scotia Sea and Drake Passage, though they were yet to be given those names, because the Sussex ghost ship arrived in those latitudes before Francis Drake. Now, seemingly endlessly, she rounded the freezing, stormy end of the world, between Antarctica and the two capes. The captain and the mate became two albatrosses, forever swooping around the carrack, and Thomas was a grey-bearded mariner, peering out through spray and spume.

It was over 300 years later, in the nineteenth century, that a Dutch ship was attempting to round the Horn, bound for Australia. She was attempting to tack into the face of a howling westerly, and the wind was continually driving her back eastwards. The first mate pleaded with the captain, Captain Vanderdecken, to go about and sail by way of the Cape of Good Hope.

'I'll go about for nothing or no one,' bellowed Vanderdecken, against the sound of wind and spray – and finally the mate and the crew attempted to wrest control of the ship from the captain. This was surely not mutiny, for he had lost his mind. 'Damn your soul to hell,' roared Vanderdecken, and drove a belaying pin right through the body of the first mate, pinning him to the main mast. 'Neither God, nor all the angels in heaven, or Satan, and all the Devils in hell, will take my command from me, or drive me from my course; I'm captain of this ship.'

And then for a while all was suddenly calm around that ship, and into that still circle sailed an ancient galleon, and on the poop deck of that galleon stood an old greybeard.

'I'll bring you a fair wind,' shouted the old greybeard, 'let me come aboard.'

… and he climbed aboard Vanderdecken's ship, and gave him a dagger, and of course it was the dagger that held the mark of Cain, the dagger he had used to slay his brother. Then the greybeard faded away, and the ancient carrack was gone, and the soul of the first mate, whose body was pinned to the main mast, slipped away – and it was not damned to hell; but Vanderdecken was damned – damned to sail endlessly round the southern ocean, round Good Hope and the Horn. He is, of course, known as the Flying Dutchman.

But maybe one day Vanderdecken will be able to pass on the dagger, the murder weapon, or maybe it would be the belaying pin he used to murder the first mate. Maybe there will be a round-the-world yacht, trying hubristically to break some record or other, rounding the Horn, and maybe Vanderdecken will get them to take the cursed relay baton.

Then it will be another vessel endlessly circling the southern latitudes of the globe; but however the story continues, not many people will know that it all began in Sussex, not so very far from Lurgashall. But you know, dear reader, and the reason you know is because I've told you.

A life on the ocean wave,
Is better than going to sea,
And if I spin a yarn to you,
You can spin a yarn to me.

POOR OLD PEGGY POYSON

The pub in Lurgashall isn't called the Flying Dutchman, but it is called Noah's Ark, which is an unusual name for an English pub. It's had that name since the eighteenth century. It has always dealt with the refreshments during Tally Nob, the midsummer fair. It was during one Tally Nob that the sexton was on his way to dig a grave in St Laurence's churchyard, when he got somewhat waylaid by the festivities; it wasn't till near on midnight that he began to dig the grave by lantern light. It is not the best of ideas to be digging graves at night, and certainly not a midsummer's night.

The sexton found that when you've got a few drinks under your belt, digging seems like harder work than usual, and he leaned on his shovel for a moment to wipe his brow. Looking up, what did he see, but a whole lot of little lights jigging about.

'Lord, it's the Pharisees,' he said to himself, before he saw that it was nine black cats, a-capering and a-jigging about on their back legs; the lights were the flashes from their eyes.

'I'll scatter you lot,' said the sexton, and reached into his pile of earth for a stone.

'Sexton,' said a voice.

'Who wants me?' said the sexton.

'I does,' said a black cat.

'Can you talk?' exclaimed the astonished sexton.

'Can you?' replied the cat sarcastically.

Now, the sexton had never had a conversation with a cat before, and he thought he'd better watch his step.

'Begging you pardon sir,' he said, 'what can I do for you?'

'I would be very much obliged,' said the cat,' if you would be good enough to tell old Dan'l Ratcliffe that poor old Peggy Poyson is dead.'

'I would be very happy to do so, sir, if I knew who Dan'l Ratcliffe was, but there ent no Dan'l Ratcliffe lives round these parts.'

'Oh yes there is,' said the cat.

'Oh no there isn't,' said the sexton – and then remembering manners and proper deference, 'Sorry sir, but I knows everyone round these parts, from yere to the Black Down, and I don't know no Dan'l Ratcliffe.'

'Yes you do,' said the cat, and then it said 'miaow', and all nine cats stalked out of the churchyard in a row.

'Oh my Lord,' said the sexton to himself, 'wife'll never believe this.'

Nor did she, after he walked back to his home in Sod's Farm and roused her from her slumbers; she was ready to fetch him one round the pate with a rolling pin.

'… there was nine cats a dancing,' he was saying.

'… and you filled your fat belly at Tally Nob … and you went a-grave digging in the middle of the night like some cockney grave robber, and …'

'… but the cat said, "Tell Dan'l Ratcliffe that poor old Peggy Poyson is dead."'

'Miaow,' said the couple's cat, standing upright on its back legs and staring at them.

The couple ceased their argument in astonishment.

'Miaow,' said the cat again, 'poor old Sussex – all the old ways be a gooin'.'

'Did you speak, Tiddles?' said the amazed wife of the amazed sexton.

'Did you?' responded the cat, fully as sarcastic as the feline in the churchyard; 'and please don't call me Tiddles, I find it most demeaning; my name is Daniel Ratcliffe, and this is very bad news.'

'Is it?'

'Is it? Is it? How could you ask? The last of the knuckers, poor old Peggy Poyson, with her frowzy, poison breath – she's gone from us. Alack and alas – no more dragons. Everything is going; you be watchful, sexton – we might lose all the elm trees, and then what will you use for coffins? I must go and gather all the cats of Sussex – and we'll have a grand funeral, and a grand wake, and a grand caterwauling for the last of the knuckers. Oh 'tis such a responsibility being king of the cats. Tiddles indeed; pah.'

Well, with those words, the sexton's cat disappeared from Sod's Farm, and was never seen anywhere round about Lurgashall again.

He is, however, king of all the cats in Sussex, so he'll have set up his court somewhere; I believe he may have lived with Halima, the lady of St Leonard's Forest, for a while. Certainly the cats of Sussex held a great funeral for the poor, last knucker. Extinctions, however, are sometimes followed by re-introductions, and, as we know, there are now some very strange creatures entering Sussex via Gatwick Airport.

The Hungry Grave

Then, in another time, there was another sexton. This sexton wouldn't be found having a few drinks at Tally Nob; he'd scowl at people, though sometimes there would be something like a smirk hovering over his lips.

Now, no gravedigger would dig a grave unless there was someone to go in it, waiting horizontal on a table, with coins on their eyes. But this sexton would dig a grave, and someone would ask, 'Who be that grave for, sexton?' and the sexton would look up, with that smirk on his lips, and say, 'Oh just ye wait and see,' and sure enough, the sexton's interlocutor would be stone dead by the following day, and lying in the grave the day after that.

Now this continued, and it has to be said that folk should really have noticed that something wasn't right, but sometimes Sussex folk are known as 'selig', or silly, and maybe this applies to the folk round about Lurgashall.

One day, a young girl looked over the wall whilst the sexton was removing his boots to take out a stone, and saw that he had cloven hooves. Oh Lord, oh lord; she daren't speak to the vicar because the vicar knew nothing of the village folk, and kept writing books, and running around with a butterfly net and such. So she walked all the way to the rickety-rackety wooden hut in Amberley Swamp, and the old woman – Old Nan – listened to the story.

'Well,' said Old Nan, appearing behind the sexton after he'd dug the grave, 'you do dig a nice, neat grave, my dear.'

The sexton wasn't used to compliments, and he waited for the inevitable question.

'Cat got your tongue?' said Old Nan.

'Miaow,' said Daniel Ratcliffe from behind a gravestone.

'Ent you going to ask?' enquired the sexton.

'Ask what?' said Old Nan.

'Who be that grave for, sexton?' said the sexton.

'Aha,' screeched Old Nan, 'take this, you gurt fool,' and she thrust a Sussex diamond into the sexton's hand.

'Oh Lord,' cried the sexton, and fell backwards into the grave and perished.

I don't know who filled the grave in, but someone did, and there never was a funeral held. As for Old Nan, she walked all the way back to Amberley Swamp; but she had a few drinks in the Noah's Ark before she did so – and they were on the house. I wonder, now I've told this story, if I could go to the Noah's Ark and get a drink on the house?

Feathers, Blood and Bone

Well, if we travel south and west from Lurgashall and Midhurst, close to the border with Hampshire, before we reach Kingley Vale and complete our widdershins circumambulation of Sussex, we come to Torberry Hill. This hill buzzes with stories; and on a midsummer night, whilst the black cats are dancing in graveyards, the Pharisees are holding their revels on Torberry.

Like so many Sussex hills, Torberry is surmounted by an Iron Age hill fort – and Torberry's hill fort is shaped like a spoon. One story has it that the Devil, after digging out the Devil's Punchbowl near Hindhead in Surrey, took a spoonful of hot punch, burnt his satanic lips, and hurled the spoon away. It landed on the top of Torberry. The Devil did seem to spend rather a lot of time digging holes.

Torberry has its buried treasure legends too; and as these stories are told throughout time, they often adopt pieces of history.

In this case the story of the escape of Charles II after the Battle of Worcester has added to the legend, for it is said locally that the escaping Royalists buried their gold there, and that the only way to retrieve it is to plough the top of the hill with a golden plough.

> He who would find what Tarberry would bear,
> Must plough it with a golden share.

As for the Pharisees, they always dance on the hill on midsummer's night – and the Fairy Bed is named after them. This is a raised bit of land, the cross-shaped base of a vanished windmill: imagine being in that windmill on midsummer's night when the Pharisees were dancing – there would surely have been a mad miller on Torberry Hill.

The derivation of the name 'Torberry' is usually given as the fort on, or near, a tor: 'tor' being the old Celtic word for a hill, or rocky peak; and 'berry' (or 'bury', as in Cissbury Ring) being a fort. However Torberry, in sedimentary Sussex, hardly looks like a rocky peak, like one of those granite tors on Dartmoor; nor a singular, pointy hill like Glastonbury Tor. As a hill, for all its commanding views, it can be quite elusive to find, hiding beneath Hemner Hill and the Harting Downs, both of which rise from the ridge of the South Downs.

It is also not pronounced as spelt; it is pronounced 'Tarberry', which sounds much more like 'Tarrble Hill'. In the Sussex dialect 'tarble' is 'terrible'; just ask the Revd W.D. Parish! In East Sussex there is a Tarble Down, which carries the history of a fierce and bloody battle, and maybe on Torberry there was once such a conflict – an ancient, pre-historic battle – and maybe the Pharisees are the remnants of these ancient people and that ancient bloodletting, for the Pharisees were never all sweetness and light.

Or maybe the hill was terrible for another reason; a place of sacrifice and fear. Whatever, whichever, whyever – there is still blood in that soil.

If you look for the path to the top of the hill you will be baffled; the footpath just goes round the hill, up a bit, down a bit. You might see a gate, though, and on that gate there is a sign: 'Buriton Estates Limited. Strictly Private. Trespassers will be prosecuted.' The top of the hill is private land, and it is used for pheasant shoots.

If you work in the city, in the financial district, it is nice sometimes to don a Barbour cap and waxed jacket and pretend to be a countryman for a while. You can blast a few pheasants out of the sky, and maybe link up with your lovely secretary in a quaint hotel in Midhurst. It makes for a very pleasant few days, and that hotel serves the most glorious Chateau Musar.

One such gentleman was on a shoot, and the beaters had just flushed the pheasants up into the air. He was ready to blast the contents of his gun up into the sky when he heard the jarring sound of a magpie that was standing on a post. For no more particular reason than the hell of it, he blasted the magpie full of lead shot. The head gamekeeper did notice, and thought to himself: 'What an arsehole,' but he didn't say anything because this man was an influential customer, and the shoot was new and still establishing its reputation.

Way, way away, though – in another place, and maybe another time – something shuddered. Daniel Ratcliffe, staying with Old Nan in Amberley Swamp, pricked up his ears and miaowed. The cockerel uttered a throaty sound, and a water vole peered out of its hole and blinked.

'What's this, what's this?' muttered Old Nan, feeling like something had just fallen out of the world. She called to her familiar – that juddering, jabbering magpie – but instead of its presence somewhere, all she felt was an emptiness. She took an alder stick and stirred a pool with it. She looked into the picture forming after the ripples ceased, and she saw Maggie Pie, lying on the ground in a mess of feathers and bones.

The old woman screeched, then she cursed and shuffled into the hut, picked up Daniel Ratcliffe, then put him down, went outside again, spat at the cockerel, walked round in a circle – then disgorged a stream of curses.

She started to collect herbs from marshy, boggy places, then mixed them and stirred, and muttered, and cursed, and a mist rose out of the swamp, and swirled around and crept off north-westwards.

That evening the magpie-slayer drove back towards Midhurst having enjoyed the day, and enjoying the sense of anticipation for what awaited him at the hotel. He decided to give the lady a call, fumbled for his iPhone, and found it missing. He swore – when something is discovered to be lost, it is so easy to realise just when and where you dropped it. He turned the BMW around and headed back for Torberry.

The summer evening shadows had lengthened as he climbed over the gate with the 'Strictly Private' sign. The Pharisees stopped dancing, and hid, and watched.

Then the magpie-slayer heard the sound of his own customised ring tone – it was playing 'Blow my Whistle', and he thought what a stroke of luck to be phoned just then, and he headed towards the sound. But he couldn't find it in the grass; just a pile of feathers and bones. He heard it again, then the juddering cackle of a magpie: 'Blow my whistle, baby – jrrrrk jrrrrk jrrrrk – Tarble Tarble. Blood and Bone. Blood and Bone.'

Surely this was some bloody kids playing tricks – it must be. He looked up and saw two great red eyes a shining. Bloody kids. Meaning not to show too much undignified anger, just a cool, collected and superior sarcasm, he said: 'Oh, what big eyes you have.'

'All the better to see you with.'

There was a terrible flapping from the bushes, and a huge pair of black and white wings. He was genuinely terrified now, and found himself compelled to utter: 'What big wings you have.'

'All the better to fold around you.'

… and then there were terrible claws, like the talons of a buzzard.

'What big claws you have.'

'All the better to grasp you with.'

… and then there was that massive, jabbing beak.

'What a big beak you have.'

'All the better to EAT YOU ALL UP WITH.'

… and then there was a flapping and a shaking, and the crunching of bone and the slurping of blood.

The young woman waited in the hotel in Midhurst, but he never showed up. Humiliated, she returned to London the next morning – but later, on being told he'd gone missing, she didn't know what to think, and certainly not what to say. It all came out in the police enquiry of course – but she wasn't a suspect, and no one was ever charged. It was rather assumed that he'd 'done a Reggie' – that act of making off into another life that became a piece of modern folklore after the fictional actions of Reginald Perrin, and the non-fictional actions of John Stonehouse.

But to use a quote from an unknown book, a quote I used in the introduction: 'As night falls, it requires very little effort for those who stand beside a downland tumulus in the screaming wind, or in the dark recesses of a wealden copse, to feel something of the religion of the pagan South Saxons, their belief in barrow wights, witch hounds and wood demons', and even in the south of England some of these places can be remote and unvisited, and if the mutilated remains of a man were to be deposited upside-down in a tree, it could be there forever without being noticed.

***

A magpie's flight could easily take us over Bow Hill and back to Kingley Vale. And we could start our widdershins perambulation all over again, and pick up more, different, stories; for the land is full of them, and however much the land may be built on, or abused, the people on that land are still full of stories. They may not be stories told to folklorists, or in front of hanging drapes and magic lanterns at storytelling festivals, but those stories are there. Without them we would only be creatures that react to stimuli, but we are *Homo Narrans* – we are creatures that try to make sense out of life by creating narrative. And if all we do is create a lot of old nonsense, then so be it; I, for one, will always like a good story.

10

Still Rambling On
The Legend at the Bottom of a Map

When you go for a walk, how do you decide where to go? Have you got a guidebook in your hand? Are you following dashed lines on a map? Are you following the instructions on one of those heritage industry sign boards?

And where will the stories be? In the guidebook? On the map (amidst all those place names so carefully collected by nineteenth-century surveyors)? Written on the sign boards?

Yes, they might well be; but they are in other places too – and sometimes they creep up and take you by surprise, or a story might lurch across the road like the Piltdown Man, and you must be attentive if you want to avoid an accident.

There is no greater guide than serendipity – the unexpected discovery, the 'happy accident' – or even the not-so-happy accident. In a Persian story, the king of Serendippo sends his three sons out into the world to learn wisdom, and they encounter the unexpected, the surprising: a one-eyed lame camel and a pregnant woman.

Now, I've never stumbled across wisdom, but I've found unexpected insights, sudden alternative view points, and a bin full of frogs.

These walks may be unplanned. A stroll through Crawley one evening, looking for an Indian restaurant, led me to get lost and to see a smudge of St Leonard's Forest through a gap in the concrete, and a reconstituting dragon in a bin.

When setting out on an exploration it is good to deliberately leave oneself open to the possibility of new discovery, rather than to accept a conventional ordering of places and events that has been taken from a book, which has in turn taken it from another book, and gives us a history and a geography that slot into a dominant and unchallenged paradigm, leaving us to trudge along like sleepwalkers, with all our senses in hibernation.

Writing in *Mythogeography*, Phil Smith, aka The Crab Man, turns a walk into a 'drift', and suggests: 'Get rid of rational way-finding! At worst use chance (dice or sticks) to determine which way to go – but best is to go by instinct.' He goes on to write:

> Allow the narrative of your walk to develop. After a while certain things may begin to connect and once that starts happening, without obsessively pursuing a story, you can begin, collectively, to 'compose' your drift, allowing what has happened so far to determine your next choices, maybe to seek out certain things, trying for entry to certain places, to accept certain affordances that help to develop what you have already found. (It doesn't always happen that a narrative emerges, and it isn't necessary, but when the offer comes encourage it to unfold.)

Even when you are being guided and controlled on your explorations, things can be viewed differently by taking the 'wrong' path. Like, for instance, going through different doors and against the ordered direction in Arundel Castle (is this like going widdershins?), noting the stories that you are being fed, but then looking at them through the eyes of different characters; and then taking more note of the stories that come from other visitors: an American woman peered down the deep, deep well, the well that General Waller emptied in 1644 to drive the inhabitants of the castle mad with thirst, and held on to her glasses, fearful they would tumble down the well. I remarked on this, and she told me about her job as an optician and her collection of 1950s American spectacles – and I drifted from the medieval heart of a largely Victorian castle to the American mid-west in the 1950s, and wondered about emigration patterns, reasons for leaving, layers of history, and the material basis of power.

ROSIE'S WALK

In a few of my Sussex perambulations I have been accompanied by a walking comrade called Rosie, and by her son Ben when he's not at school. It was Ben who picked up a shard of yew bark in Kingley Vale and told me it was a dragon scale.

One time Rosie and I drove into an area of Sussex close to the border with Hampshire, and thought that we would travel randomly – just see what we would see. With dark clouds and that clearly defining bright sun that shines occasionally as rain threatens, we passed through beautiful hilly woodland from West Marden to Walberton, until we found ourselves on the flat land north of the A27, land afflicted by that post-agricultural, post-industrial drab ennui that afflicts so much of the world. Even the motorist can be pixie-led, though the pixies may be riding on spectral motor scooters like a bunch of whimsical, diminutive mods, and after we'd passed the Defence and Evaluation Research Agency's Model Antenna Range on Common Road (a road that no longer passes any common land) for the third time, we really began to think that our excursion was a mistake.

Then, at Aldsworth, Rosie noticed a tower on a hill. There's our target, we thought; we'll walk to it. We wandered down a country road, or rather Rosie strode down it whilst I trotted along behind like a tired hobbit, and came across a tiny twelfth-century downland church, the church of Saint Peter, Racton with Lordington. From inside the church the entrance appeared to be within a wardrobe, so stepping back out of the church entailed entering a wardrobe and stepping out into the wondrous land of Sussex, far more interesting in the complexity of its story than Narnia.

In the church there were lots of references to the Gunter family, and there was a statue of Sir George and Lady Ursula Gunter, with Sir George bare-headed; hardly surprising, because his helmet and a gauntlet that looked like a woolly hat were hanging from high up on the wall, looking like kitsch mementos from a Christmas shop.

Rosie and I sat in the churchyard to read gravestone inscriptions, eat sandwiches and drink tea, when, inevitably, it started to rain. We put up our umbrellas, and, feeling somewhat competitive, had a cherry stone flobbing competition; who could flob the most stones into the lid of the flask at five yards?

Behind us, on the hill, was that singular, and somewhat sinister, tower.

The rain eased, and we headed towards the tower. It was a tall, eerie-looking eighteenth-century folly, gazing hollow-eyed towards the sea. In it there were two youths with rucksacks, which looked like they contained aerosol cans. They mumbled incoherently at my annoyingly cheery 'hello', silently willing us to go away so they could commence their graffiti.

Beyond the tower we discovered a sunken lake and a hidden garden, and then we looked over a gate for a surprising view – rolling parkland leading down to a grand Edwardian country mansion, Stansted House. I was surprised, because, as with the Amberley marshes, I was connecting two geographies. Stansted House is in Hampshire and I have been employed to tell stories there, my route to the house taking me through Havant and Leigh Park – an urban sprawl north of Portsmouth. The linear view of the land we get from roads put Stansted House, in my mental map, in quite a different place than the Sussex downland around Funtington and Lordington. I looked with fresh eyes.

And later, when I researched the places we had been, I discovered that the Gunter family had been heavily involved in the escape of King Charles II, something that connected me with Ainsworth's novel, *Ovingdean Grange*, a version of the story of the Devil's Dyke, that long distance footpath, the Monarch's Way; and Trevor's Boots.

The tower was Racton Folly, a folly that Mark Hoult accurately describes in his Sussex website as having a 'Blair Witch Project-type feel' to it, and I discovered a whole raft of stories about the tower. But they're not in this book – because this is, after all, the final chapter, so we're very nearly finished. I'll have to put those stories in another book!

But in the end, it isn't those written stories that are important; it is the places, the walking, the people you meet, and the stories they tell.

I think we must finish with a story – and the last word will go to Old Nan.

Tell Me a Story

Once upon a time a traveller got lost; pixie-led in the night, in a marsh mist, out on Amberley Swamp. He stumbled around until, through the mist, he saw a rickety-rackety wooden hut.

He knocked on the door.

'Hello my dear,' said Old Nan. 'What be you dooin' out yere, on a misty-moisty night?'

'I'm looking for shelter,' said the traveller. 'Please could I take shelter for the night?'

'Oh, come on in,' fussed the old woman, 'sit down there by the fire.'

He sat in front of the fire, and the old woman said, 'You looks cold and wet and hungry, I 'spect you'd want something to eat and something to drink.'

She gave him some bread and some very strange-tasting cheese, and then she produced a jug of huckle-my-puff. Ooooh, that was better; it warmed him through to his bones.

'Now,' she said, 'I haven't seen a soul for I don't know how long, and I've heard no news, and I've heard no stories; would you have a story to tell?'

'Stories?' said the traveller. 'Oh I've no time for stories; they are foolish things for children.'

'A story, just a story – I'm only asking for a story,' exclaimed the old woman.

'No, I don't mean to be rude, but I've no time for stories,' said the traveller, who plainly was being rude.

'Well, maybe you'll sit there, and I can tell you a story.'

'No, no, just show me where I can sleep the night.'

'Oh very well,' said the old woman angrily, and she took him out of the hut and showed him a lean-to attached to the wall. There was some straw and blankets on the floor, and hanging from a hook on the ceiling was a dead pig. This didn't bother him – you have to hang your meat somewhere – and he curled up on the floor amidst the straw and blankets.

It must have been midnight when he woke up, because it usually is midnight when things happen in stories. There was a scrabbling at the door, and the handle started to turn. The traveller buried himself beneath the straw and blankets, just before the door creaked open and the room was filled with a cold bluish light.

In came Lord Moon. 'Yum, piggy-wiggy, crackling, porky-worky,' said Lord Moon. 'I wants, so I shall have.'

He reached up, took the dead pig off the hook, and, holding it over his roundy shoulder, disappeared back out the door.

The traveller stuck his head out of the straw and blankets. 'Oh Lord, what's to be done? I can't take the pig off that terrible creature, but I can't do nothing or the old woman will think 'twas

I that stole the pig, like some Fulking farmer on Beeding Hill with a pig in a poke.'

So he decided to follow Lord Moon. Outside, the vapours of mist had drifted away, leaving a clear dark night, with the stars twinkling in the sky, and he followed the pale light of the spectre. He followed till Lord Moon reached the banks of the Arun, and then the creature turned round and gazed straight at the traveller.

'Hungry,' said Lord Moon, and opened his moony mouth showing layers of sharp teeth, like that king of the river, the pike.

'YUM,' he screeched, and hurtled towards the terrified traveller who turned and ran, flinging himself into a freezing ditch, where he crouched with the water up to his nose.

'Where are you, where are you? – I'm hungry,' called Lord Moon, flitting up and down the edge of the ditch.

Finally it was the first grey light of morning, and Lord Moon was gone. The traveller tried to scrabble his way out of the ditch, but his freezing fingers just slipped through the gubbery hike, the stinking mud, until he saw an alder tree with the roots trailing over the edge of the ditch.

He caught hold of a root, and slowly – slowly – hauled himself up until SNAP, the root broke, and he fell back.

Back onto the straw and blankets – and hanging from the hook above him was the dead pig.

The door opened and in came the old woman.

'Well,' she said, 'did you have a good night's sleep?'

'NO, I did not,' cried the traveller. 'I had a dream that a horrible creature, worse than the most hideous Wealden Willock, came and stole the pig, and I went off after it, and …'

Well the long and the short of it, dear reader, is that the traveller told Old Nan the same story that I've just told you, and she said to him, 'Well, I don't know if it was the huckle-my-puff, or if it was the cheese, but you've just told me a story. So now, if you accept someone's hospitality and they ask for a story, you have got a story to tell.'

And so he did; he would tell that story, and over time it changed. And he told it to someone who told it to someone else, who told it to someone else and on and on, till someone told it to me. At least I think they did. So if you, dear reader, want to tell that story, you can. But it'll change, because that's what stories do – your personality will go into the story, and it'll become yours.

And follow your feet – because that's where your heart is, though I'm not sure if it's in the left foot or the right foot.

My little book ends right here,
So I'm off down the pub for a pint of beer.

GLOSSARY

Blumber: The spoken equivalent of male bovine effluent.

Bostal: A steep pathway up a hill, and, if travelling the
                   other way, a steep pathway down a hill.

Danelaw: When Sussex was Saxon, the Danelaw was a
                   benighted northern wasteland stretching from
                   the Midlands to Yorkshire over which the so-
                   called laws of the Danes held sway.

Ellet: Elder tree.

Elynge: Solitary, far from the neighbours, uncanny, eerie.

Frowzy: Scruffy and a bit stinky.

Mawkin: Scarecrow.

Mumpers: Tramps; for example, travellers in carts supposedly
                   not leading a gypsy life, and looked down upon by
                   those who considered themselves true gypsies or
                   didicais.

Old Gooseberry: Old Nick; he who cannot creep between the oak
                   and its bark.

Owlers: Export smuggler; usually smuggling wool. He who
                   supports his own entrepreneurial initiative.

Poke: A long sack.

Pokeputte: A longer sack.

Quotted: Glutted.

Scudder: Good all-rounder of a horse, bred by the Romani people for road racing.

Selig: Silly, meaning happy or blessed. The silly fool may really be the holy fool.

Shoolers: Idle, lazy fellows.

Shrammed: Benumbed with cold.

Spronkett: I dunno, but it doesn't sound very polite.

Twaddling: Foolish chatter.

Willock: A wild man, one from the Weald, a wildisher; a mad man; a mad or wild (out of control) animal.

Wildisher: A Willock who is more willocky than the average willock.

BIBLIOGRAPHY

BOOKS

Ainsworth, W. Harrison, *Ovingdean Grange: A Tale of the South Downs* (Various publishers, originally published 1857)

Arscott, David, *The Little Book of Sussex* (The History Press, 2011)

Boogaart, Pieter, *A272: An Ode to a Road* (Pallas Athene Ltd, 2000)

Bowen, Pat, *20 Sussex Walks* (Snake River Press, 2007)

Brooks J.A., *Railway Ghosts* (Jarrold, 1985)

Campbell, John, 'Remembering Patrick Kavanagh', in *A Sense of Love, A Sense of Place* (Adare Press, 1992)

Deakin, Roger, *Wildwood: A Journey Through Trees* (Penguin Books, 2007)

Doyle, Ursula (ed.), *Love Letters of Great Women* (Macmillan, 2009)

Ghosh, Durba, *Sex and the Family in Colonial India: The Making of Empire* (Cambridge University Press, 2006)

Glyn, Philip J. & Prendergast, Hew D.V., *Ashdown Forest: An Illustrated Guide* (Essedon Press, 1995)

Goodhall, John, *Pevensey Castle* (English Heritage, 1999; revised reprint 2011)

Hutchins, Pat, *Rosie's Walk* (The Bodley Head, 1968)

Jennings, Louis John, *Field Paths and Green Lanes: Being Country Walks, Chiefly in Surrey and Sussex* (Historical Print Editions, 2011; originally published 1877)

Lucas, E.V., *Highways and Byways in Sussex* (Macmillan & Co., Ltd, 1904)

MacFarlane, Robert, *The Old Ways: A Journey on Foot* (Hamish Hamilton, 2012)

Mee, Arthur, *The King's England: Sussex* (Hodder and Stoughton, 1937)

Meynell, Esther, *The County Books: Sussex* (Robert Hale Ltd, 1947)

Moore, J., *Sussex Legends and Folklore* (James Pike Ltd, 1976)

O'Leary, Michael, *Hampshire and Isle of Wight Folk Tales* (The History Press, 2011)

Oliver, Neil, *A History of Ancient Britain* (Weidenfield & Nicolson, 2011)

Parish, Revd W.D., *A Dictionary of the Sussex Dialect and Collection of Provincialisms in use in the County of Sussex* (Originally published by Farncombe & Co., 1875)

Ritson, Joseph, 'A Dissertation on Fairies', in *Folk-Lore and Legends: English* (J.B. Lippincott Company, 1891)

Rudd-Jones, Nicholas & Stewart, David, *Pathways* (Guardian Books, 2011)

Simpson, Jacqueline, *Folklore of Sussex* (revised addition, Tempus Publishing, 2002; originally published 1973)

Smith, Phil, *Mythogeography, A Guide to Walking Sideways* (Triarchy Press, 2010)

Staines, Revd E. Noel, *Dear Amberley: A Guide to Amberley and History of the Parish* (published for Amberley Parochial Church Council, 1968; reprinted 1998)

Westwood, Jennifer & Simpson, Jacqueline, *The Lore of the Land: A Guide to England's Legends, from Spring-heeled Jack to the Witches of Warboys* (Penguin Books, 2005)

Wymer, Norman, *Companion into Sussex* (Methuen & Co. Ltd, 1950)

CD

Collins, Shirley, *Adieu to Old England*

WEBSITES

http://books.google.co.uk/books?id=0l_k-XMIiQIC&printsec=fr
   ontcover#v=onepage&q&f=false, containing *Zuplo's Dictionary
   of Weights and Measures for the British Isles: The Middle Ages to
   the Twentieth Century*

http://www.birdman.org.uk/go/page? History of the Bognor
   Birdman competition.

http://www.british-history.ac.uk/report.aspx?compid=43540

http://www.britishpathe.com/video/downs-ranger

http://ebba.english.ucsb.edu/ballad/20258/xml

http://en.wikipedia.org/wiki/Sussex

http://en.wikipedia.org/wiki/Sussex_dialect#Words_for_mud

http://jbleitz.com/legends.html

http://www.michaelolearystoryteller.com

http://www.monarchsway.50megs.com/index.html

http://www.novareinna.com/romani/horse.html

http://www.sussexarch.org.uk/saaf/folklist.html

http://web.iiit.ac.in/~nirnimesh/Literature/sparrows.htm

http://www.westsussex.info/about.shtml

http://www.youtube.com/watch?v=6aPETwG5HyA

MAPS

Ordnance Survey Landranger Series: 186-189, 197-199

If you enjoyed this book, you may also be interested in …

Berkshire Folk Tales

DAVID ENGLAND & TINA BILBÉ

This collection, inspired by the folklore of the Royal County, contains a plethora of tales robustly retold for a contemporary audience. The exploits of well-known figures such as Herne the Hunter and Dick Turpin feature alongside many of the county's lesser-known legends. Berkshire Folk Tales is a heady mix of blood-thirsty, funny, passionate and moving stories.

978 0 7524 6745 0

Worcestershire Folk Tales

DAVID PHELPS

From battles of the Civil War to witchcraft trials, Worcestershire is steeped in history – and almost every village has some dark tale of magical events to tell. Ordinary folk from all walks of life mix with devils, ogres and ghosts. Complemented by beautiful illustrations, Worcestershire Folk Tales is crammed with these myths, legends and mysterious yarns.

978 0 7524 8580 5

Suffolk Folk Tales

KIRSTY HARTSIOTIS

With its wild eroding sea, gentle rolling fields and tall churches, Suffolk is a county of contrasts. It may seem a kindly and civilised place, but down dark town streets, lurk strange beasts, ghosts and tricksters. These traditional tales take you into a hidden world of green children and wildmen, of lovers from beyond the grave, of demonic black dogs …

978 0 7524 6747 4

Visit our website and discover thousands of other History Press books.

www.thehistorypress.co.uk